In Praise Of
Free Parking

"**Alan Dickson** measures riches in terms of leisure time spent with family and friends. He'd like to help you do the same."---- *The Globe and Mail*

"**Free Parking** is classically contrarian, flying in the face of every bit of self-serving wisdom to today's vendors of mutual funds, banking products and insurance dispense about retirement in Canada" ----*The National Post*

"**Alan Dickson** is living large on less. And how he does it has repercussions and perhaps hope for all those would - be early retirees, rat race runners and toxic-job holders who dream of finding a way out." ----*Vancouver Province*

"**His views** provoke controversy as they go beyond the accepted wisdom of financial management."---- *Victoria Times Colonist*

ADVANCE TO GO!

THE ROAD TO A RICH RETIREMENT

ALAN DICKSON

PREFERRED MARKETING INC

National Library of Canada Cataloguing in Publication Data

Dickson, Alan, 1951 -
Advance To Go; The Road To A Rich Retirement

Includes bibliographical references.
ISBN 0-9688855-1-9

1. Retirement--Planning. 2 Retirement income--Planning.
3. Finance, Personal. 4. Investments 1. Title
HG179.D4488 2003   332.024'01   C2003-910722-1

Published By:
Preferred Marketing Inc.
870 Government St.
Duncan, B.C. V9L 1B6

Printed in Canada

TO MY FAMILY

THANK YOU

To the readers of Free Parking who took the time to chat when I was visiting their local book stores. To those who telephoned, wrote and e-mailed their comments and encouragement and yes — their stories of successfully living on less income.

To the journalists of local and national newspapers and magazines, to the producers and hosts of talk shows and news programs who looked past the grammatical flaws, saw the story, and helped get the message out.

To the book sellers who responded to inquiries from their customers and ordered and reordered beyond my expectations.

To family and friends who listened patiently, to yet another conversation centred on Free Parking, while hiding (usually) signs of boredom.

Table of Contents

1

PREFACE

"The Almighty Dollar, that
great object of universal devotion
throughout our land." ...Washington Irving

There wasn't suppose to be a second book. Come to
think of it, I never planned on writing the first. Ask any of
the editors who struggled through *Free Parking* dodging
past typos and grammatical blunders or stumbling over
dangling participles or particles or whatever. I lay full
responsibility at the feet of the publishers of the countless
financial planning books and articles. This steady barrage
of glorified advertising by the banks, investment dealers,
and insurance companies thinly disguised as investment
advice.

I was quite content with my routine. Working three
or four days a week, with a few weeks off over the winter to
find someplace warm and a few more in the summer to go
sailing. But not writing. I was tinting windows. At least I

was for the past decade. Before that it was selling investments and insurance and the decade before that, cleaning floors. It was all the same to me. Do a good job, make a decent income and then get back to living. Work is part of the "living" but only a small part. I had been living this way for over thirty years and there was no reason to change ... but ... but the constant badgering about needing all this money to retire or else....

And there was no one saying: "It isn't true!" So... I decided to say it — and now — I'm an author.

But it was only going to be one book, *Free Parking*. In six months I'd have sold (or stored) most of my copies and I could go back to tinting windows. The following summer I'd be back sailing. And of course, at the risk of repetition, there was never any intention of a follow-up. I said my piece. The financial planning business, indeed, the whole consumerism society, has pushed us too far. The idea that happiness, success and fulfillment are somehow related to how much money we make or what assets we have gathered around us is absurd. It's time to reject the big income, the big house and, most of all, the big retirement savings plan.

Still, there are some doubters. I'm not surprised. The leaders of business, politics, and special interest groups have long ago determined that if you say something often enough and loud enough, eventually many will consider it true. Nothing has been said louder or more often than the message that we live in the greatest part of the world, and our greatness is shown by all the wealth we have. Now, to have those statements challenged is not to be taken lightly. It's only reasonable that there should be those who doubt, indeed scoff, at the very notion that less can be better.

Shortly after the first article appeared in *The National Post* about *Free Parking* and my lifestyle, I knew there would have to be a second book. I've got some explaining to do.

It would not have been necessary in a previous generation. Why, the TV dads from *My Three Sons* and *Leave it to Beaver* would have easily persuaded their boys that money wasn't all that important. Jimmy Stewart and Andy Griffiths would shake their heads over the idea of working overtime for the big retirement while your younguns were at home fending for themselves. But that was a long time ago. Before the television shows of the rich and powerful. Before the movies where the stars chanted: "Greed is good!" And the self-help books assured us that God wants you and me to be rich. Who am I to argue with the likes of Michael Douglas and God? Never mind that for 2000 years men have been quoting the biblical saying: "The love of money is the root of evil", and many have lived their lives in accordance with that advice. Now these latter-day prophets are telling us that we were wrong.

Imagine if *Free Parking* had been written in the days of Plato or Aristotle. The aristocrats would have taken issue with my idea of working less. They favoured doing **no** paid work. Aristotle said, without the trace of a smile: "All paid jobs absorb and degrade the mind." But for the most part, I would have been ignored; for everyone was speaking of early retirement and shorter work weeks in the days of the Greek empire. At least all the freemen. Work was considered a curse, demeaning, to be reluctantly accomplished by slaves. Aside from brief periods in the nation of Israel, work for most of mankind's history has been viewed as a necessary evil. A brief interruption in living while one cares for the gathering of food or constructing shelter. Then — back to life. The very idea of making excessive profits had been frowned upon, even outlawed. No Microsoft for the Romans or Greeks (I said Greeks not Geeks).

We can thank John Calvin for the mess we have today. While his buddy Martin Luther was uncovering a Catholic scandal (some things don't change), Calvin was fleshing out his theory of pre-destination. He preached that most of mankind was destined to be damned. A few elite would be rewarded with eternal life and God would reveal to all who the chosen were by how much money they could make. Anyone not occupied with work gave evidence of being one of the damned. His teachings were not lost on the likes of John D. Rockefeller who piously stated: "I believe that the power to make money is a gift from God." Of course you weren't allowed to enjoy the money. John Calvin wasn't big on enjoyment and his disciple J. D. Rockefeller rarely smiled in public. You couldn't even publicly flaunt your wealth. The art of flaunting ones wealth would not be perfected for several hundred years — until our generation.

But we don't live in the days of Plato, Calvin, or sadly, even Jimmy Stewart. This is the information age, and much of the information is about money and how to get it. How to get more of it. How to hide it from the tax man while waving it in front of your neighbour. And if you can't take it with you, well you can still control the purse strings with trusts and executors. Many have been persuaded to believe in money as our only security for the future. Some have read *Free Parking* or seen a story about a simplified lifestyle and wondered, "Could I really live like that?" I'll go so far as to say you could do even better if you wanted to. Why do I say this? One of the neat things about writing a book is that you get to meet people.

Here's where most authors of financial books relate how their writings have captured the imagination of Canadians and they have been in constant demand ever since to give lectures and conduct workshops, helping you, the grateful public, to become wealthy. At the risk of sounding bitter, or at least envious, I must confess that my dance card is not full. Indeed my speaking engagements are as scarce as mutual funds making money in 2002.

If you are puzzled by this anomaly, let me assure you that I am not. Can you imagine a member of the financial community inviting me to speak to potential investors? Or what about a company trying to motivate their employees? "Nice move, Barnaby, bringing that guy Dickson in to speak to the staff. What was his topic again? 'Say goodbye to your boss and start living'. Oh yeah, the boss wants to see you. I think he's going to give you a chance to start living."

Now, where was I? Oh yes. Forget the speaking tour. But I did meet hundreds of you. Travelling across much of Canada, visiting dozens of bookstores and speaking on numerous talk shows, the greatest surprise for me was that in every area there were folks that stopped by to tell me how they were living on very little income and having the time of their lives. I heard from seniors who assured me that despite earning much less than when they were employed, they have more disposable income now than when they were working. I started jotting down stories. Others phoned or wrote letters and e-mails. And I made notes. For in these stories is the genesis of this book. I've been inspired by average people like you and your neighbours who have chosen to think for yourselves about retirement and finances. But, more importantly, you have been thinking about families and friends and communities. Early on, as you started speaking out, I knew I wanted to tell your story. You are the real heroes. You have discovered the secret to a rich retirement. Riches not measured in income and assets.

I've been searching for the best way to tell the stories from the hundreds of people that I have spoken with. Sometimes it was only a line in a conversation that lingered with me after you left. Like a smooth stone picked up while walking on a secluded beach. Months later as you stroke the stone you can see yourself walking the beach. You can feel the sand between your toes, the sun on your back, hear the sounds of the waves and the birds, smell the sea. Many of you are too modest to have your names in print and so you've been renamed. Some of the individuals you read about will have characteristics from several that I have met. I couldn't possibly introduce you all; but it was too difficult to leave any of you behind, and so, like many of today's communities, I have blended you together. You will have no trouble seeing yourself. You're the one with the white hat and the marshal's star. You're the hero.

I want you to share the thrill I had in speaking with each of you. Imagine if it was possible to gather all of you together. What a wealth of practical financial information and living skills that you could present.

Meet Charles Henderson. You may already know him, for he's alot like you. There's Charlie who likes and believes almost everyone. But there's another side, the more serious Charles who looks after the cheque book and tends to be a skeptic. And, like many of us, there's a constant conversation between the two. Thankfully few people hear us talking to ourselves, but we get to listen in on the Charlie/Charles debate. And like many of us, Charles worries about money for retirement. A few days of research and some unexpected visitors will change the way he looks at money and life. The circumstances under which Charlie and his wife meet the other participants are fictional, but be assured that the stories they all tell are real.

For those of you who have read *Free Parking,* you know my affection for the board game Monopoly. There are so many metaphors with life that can be extracted from the game. I am sure that is why it continues to be such a world-wide favourite. Now consider the space on the board marked GO. If retirement is the beginning of the next round of our life, let's call Charlie's journey in search of a rich retirement, ***Advance to Go!***

1

EMPTY PROMISES

"Do not toil to gain riches...For without fail
it makes wings for itself like those of an eagle
and flies away..".....Proverbs 23:5

"It outta be a law, that every personal finance or
'how to invest' book must begin with the phrase: 'Once
Upon a Time'. No wait! Not just the books. Every
application for an investment account, every mutual fund
prospectus, every piece of advertising: from the happy
prosperous couple sitting on a tropical beach to the graph
on the wall of your local bank showing the investment
funds going to 'infinity and beyond' — yes every
inducement for you to part with your money must begin
with that age old phrase that lets everyone know that it's
just a fairy tale."

Charles Henderson was not a happy man. After
watching his co-workers at the mill reap huge returns in
their retirement plans over the past half-decade, he had

gingerly tested the waters. In June of 1999 he opened a self directed RRSP with an investment firm, transferring in $10,000. Three months later he rolled over the bulk of his savings. He had slept very little since.

"And when your professional financial advisor starts to rattle off potential rates of return of the product that he is selling, you must be able to look behind him on the wall and see his licence that begins with the phrase: 'Once Upon a Time'. And then you know that it's only 'make believe'.

"Maybe then I could understand why that blue chip investment turned sour. It wasn't supposed to be like that. I was being careful. No risky speculation for me. After all, this is my life — and even more importantly — this is my money!"

"Give it a rest!" Harry McDougall had been listening for the past two years about Charlie's retirement woes. "Everyone is investing and they're all making tons of money. Sure we hit a little bump on the way up. But that's all it is. It just so happened, that the bump arrived the same time your money did. What are you going to do, launch a formal inquiry?"

"Never! That would only identify me. Everyone would know that I lost money — maybe I'd get the blame for the current demise in the market. You always said there was a black cloud hovering over my head. And as you said: "Everyone else is happily cashing in their winnings." Charlie paused to drain his glass. " Besides, complaining isn't manly. 'You pay your money and you take your chances'. But hold on Harry, there wasn't suppose to be any chances. That's why I went to this money expert. I read all of the testimonials from wealthy clients; I spent hours studying the charts showing the impressive returns that he garnered for those lucky enough to have him look after their money."

"So you're down some money — okay, so you're down lots of money, but is that a good enough reason to trash the whole investment community? What makes you think that your money's gone? All you have to do is hang in. Remember, Chuck, we're in for the long haul. And if you cash in now...well ..... it's your loss."

"The voice of reason. Yeah, you're probably right... as usual. Look, I gotta go. And seeing as I'm the guy who's losing money, you can get the tab."

It was the first smile Harry had seen all evening. It was worth the money to see his old friend lighten up a bit. He'd known Charlie Henderson forever. Maybe longer. They had been buds since the first grade. There had been dreams of doing great things. Setting up a business, travelling the world, saving the planet. The dreams would change as often as the tide, but they were their dreams and great fun. They'd spent every summer together, except for the two years that Charlie had gone off to Alberta. He was only gone a week and he called to say he'd found a job for Harry, and he should be on the next bus. Of course there was no way that Harry could go, seeing as he already had a job at the service station. It was a long two years, but Charlie finally came home. Only he brought a girl back with him and that changed everything. Harry had been pretty sore with Charlie. And Charlie had known all too well what Harry would think about his best friend getting married and ruining all their dreams. That's why he got married and didn't even tell his best friend.

Harry had tried staying mad for the better part of a

month. It had been no use. You couldn't stay mad with
Charlie. Well some of the guys could. Not with Charlie but
with Charles. Most of the guys thought there was just one
Charlie Henderson, but Harry knew differently. He knew
there were two even when they were in grade school. There
was Charlie who was a regular guy, and then, there was
Charles. Harry figured it out after seeing the movie about
Dr. Jeckel and Mr. Hyde. Harry liked them both but Charlie
was a lot more fun. Charles was much too serious. The way
he was always talking about saving money and being a wise
consumer. Poor Eddy. He sat next to Charlie in school and
got an ear full. And how Charlie would get real serious and
want everyone to call him Charles — even in the first grade.
Justin Cooper would make fun of ol' Charlie and they'd
start fighting. Well it wasn't much of a fight, cause Charlie
was the smallest kid in class, and Justin's mom used to buy
him clothes from the Husky section of the Eaton's
catalogue.

Yeah, some of the guys still think Charles is a pain in
the butt. But not Harry. It wasn't just that Charlie had the
best schemes for getting out of Mr. Fletcher's history class,
or that Charles would help him with his math assignments.
No. Charlie was always there to do stuff with. He was
steady, dependable, not like the kids that would drop you
like a little sister the minute some new fella came along
with a new bike. Charlie was loyal — except this one time
that he'd gone off and got married. When Harry got to know
more about Louise, he reckoned why Charlie had done it.
Why even Charles couldn't object to Louise. Harry had
done the only thing sensible. He'd gone out and got married
too.

In the early years, the weekends had the wives

shopping for kids' stuff and making plans for camping. Charlie and Harry would be watching a game on television, eating hot dogs, washing them down with beer. Now they were empty nesters and the wives had them all dieting. Talk was more often about chiropractors, dental plans, and cholesterol levels. Their plans for saving the world were interrupted by trips to the washroom. Not that it mattered, for the bold ideas of youth were now tempered with expressions of doubt and fear.

He watched Charlie slide off the bar stool and head for the door, then decide on a quick detour to the men's room. The step wasn't as quick as he remembered. The stride wasn't as long. Harry waited for Charlie to proceed outside, laid a twenty on the counter, waved to Bert behind the bar, and followed Charlie out.

"Go home and get some sleep Chuck, and I'll see you in the morning."

"Not me Buddy. Tomorrow's Saturday. You better go home and sleep it off. And I'm gone all next week. Louise is hauling me across the country to see her family."

~

Charlie stood in front of the bathroom mirror brushing his teeth, or what was left of them. Three years ago he needed a partial plate, and there were signs that it would soon need enlarging to replace the two teeth that were candidates for extraction. He combed his hand through his hair that had been retreating faster than a politician's promise after an election. Never mind. Some of the hair hadn't deserted, just taken up new residence in his ears. He made a half turn and took two steps over to the scales, and confirmed his suspicions. The two beers he had this evening had done wonders to eliminate the effects of the diet Louise had him on. Ten years ago he could eat and drink with impunity. Here was a man who should be seriously thinking of retirement. At the rate his body was deteriorating, if he wanted any golden years they would have to be enjoyed soon. But with his savings in a free fall, retirement was further away than ever.

He crawled into bed, but sleep was out of the question. He should have known better. Whenever he talked — or even thought — about his retirement funds before he went to bed, sleep was surely to be delayed by several hours. As he lay there, his mind continue to plod through the events surrounding his fateful decision to enter the stock market. How did he get himself into such a fix? He had no business being mixed up in the market. He couldn't handle uncertainty.

Even as a boy, Charles had to have everything planned, organized. If he didn't know, days in advance, everyone who would be at a party, he wouldn't go. What if Justin had been invited? They were sworn enemies. Or that new girl in grade six? What if she was there and asked him to dance? No it would be better to stay home than take the risk.

Take the risk, the words echoed in his mind. Here he was, five years away from his planned retirement, and he had taken risk. Enormous risk. With all his liquid assets. He had carefully, methodically, built a sizeable RRSP. Sizeable for the crowd that Charles Henderson hung out with. And he had done it without risk. Twenty-six years of carefully saving with GICs and Canada Savings Bonds.

"No risk!" he had stated whenever he talked to the people at Island Savings Credit Union when they occasionally inquired about his investment choices. But something had happened. Something very sinister. He sat upright in bed, startled as the words crept out from the shadows of his mind. Yes sinister. It happened at work. At least it was at the place of his employment.

"I wish now I had been working, instead of taking the two hours off to attend that seminar." he muttered to himself, but audible enough that Louise half awoke and murmured;

"Did you say something Charlie?"

"No — nothing — go back to sleep."

He continued the monologue, silently, relating the details of past events. Harrison Pulp had changed their pension plan with the blessing of the union. There would no longer be a defined pension based on years worked and salary earned. From now on each employee would manage his funds in a company sponsored RRSP copied after their U.S. operations. Most of the employees greeted the news with open arms. They welcomed the opportunity to show their investing skills. Charles figured the company wanted to cut the employees loose. The market had provided a surplus in their pension fund and Harrison Pulp was quick to get their hands on it. It was RRSP season, February 1999. The company had arranged for a financial planner to conduct a workshop on investing. The mood was festive. The stock market was hot, making new highs every other week. Everyone was deep into equity funds. Everyone but Charles. 'No risk.' he had resolutely declared when he was asked about his investing strategy. Then it happened.

Charles Henderson had been confronted with undeniable logic. He remembered every detail about Mr. Pattersen, the financial planner. He certainly looked

successful. He had arrived in a Lexus. His Harry Rosen suit
had absorbed the faint smell of new leather from the car's
interior. He had removed his suit jacket during his
presentation, revealing a watch that elicited the whisper
"Rolex" from some of the more vocal attendees. But it was
the performance that captured the hearts of his audience.
He had related how his father had died suddenly, leaving
the family destitute. How his mother had held down two
low paying jobs to keep her children from being seized by
social services. How he had vowed on his father's grave to
make a better life, not just for his family, but for all he came
in contact with; and through the miracle of mutual funds,
he was fulfilling that vow. The audience had sat wide eyed
and terrified as he exposed the evil of inflation. It had been
at this point of his performance that he had singled out
Charles.

"I agree with Charlie!" Pattersen began.

"Call him Charles when you're talking about his
money," someone yelled, to the delight of the group.

"You don't want much risk in your plan," Pattersen
continued. "But Charles *you* are taking the risk!"

He had been stunned. "I'm in guaranteed income
certificates. Guaranteed!" He had insisted. "No risk."

"Yes they are guaranteed." Pattersen began,
choosing his words. "But not without risk. You see, interest
rates are low, very low. In fact they're hardly above
inflation. When you take into account the tax liability that
you are creating inside your RRSP, I can say without a
doubt that you are losing real purchasing power, falling
behind inflation. At the same time, your colleagues here
have invested in assets that are growing by far more than
inflation. Why, the mutual funds that I have many of my

clients in, grew by more than 20% last year. Yes Charles, your money is guaranteed all right. *Guaranteed to lose* and that's risk."

He had spoken with the zeal of a television evangelist, with similar results. The room had erupted in applause, followed by the outpouring of employee pension money and additional savings into the waiting arms of their savior. It was all Charlie could do, to stop from running up to the stage with money in hand and beg, "Save me from inflation for I have sinned! Deliver me from the temptation of GICs!"

Over the next several months, Charles had pondered over the situation and watched from the sidelines as the stock market shot further and further into the stratosphere, taking with it the mutual funds that Harry and the rest of the guys had bought. Conversation at work was now dominated by discussions about net asset values and management expense ratios. These louts, who knew nothing about finances and investments. But now.... now they were investors, players in the market. They sat in the lunch room dropping names: Lynch, Soros, and Buffett. "Umph" he had thought when the names first surfaced, "The only Buffett these guys knew about until recently was Jimmy, and he talked about margaritas not Microsoft."

Unlike most of his friends, Charles knew something about money. He was not an eleventh hour convert. He had been the one who faithfully stuck to his paper route long after his buddies had declared their distaste for the nickels and dimes. His bank book had been his badge of honour which he proudly displayed to a few of his closest class-mates. He was the one who declined, after calculating the costs, to join the various drinking parties; while the only concern of the others was finding someone who looked the part to buy the illicit booze.

Maybe— and he didn't like entertaining the idea — maybe, that was why he decided to finally plunge into the murky waters of mutual funds? Could it be, that it was more than the thought of falling behind inflation? Had *No Risk Charles* been lured into losing 30 percent of his retirement savings because he wanted to be in the loop. He had always been the guy that the others had turned to when they had questions about money. "Should I lock in my mortgage for 5 years or take a variable rate? Are CSBs still a good choice or are GICs better?" The questions had stopped when the guys started outpacing Charlie with their return on investments. Worse, now he found himself on the receiving end of advice, and he knew it 'was better to give than receive'. Yes he had entered the game, determined to once again assume his role as financial confidant to the guys at the mill.

There was a crease across Charles' forehead as he recounted this part of the saga. The makings of a scowl. It was all good and well for him to be taken in by Pattersen — if his suspicions were correct. Pattersen was obviously a pro, skilled at deceiving the masses with his double-talk. But this new revelation, that his subconscious just introduced, was more disturbing. Had he really allowed his vanity to spring the trap that Pattersen had set?

It was impossible to stay in bed. He was in such a state that to remain still was out of the question, let alone trying to sleep. He would get up and go for a walk. Perhaps his legs could keep pace with his mind. He could carry on this conversation with himself without waking Louise.

~

"What happened to you last night?" Louise asked over lunch. There had been no breakfast; at least for Charles who spent the morning in bed.

"Oh, I couldn't sleep, so I went for a walk." He had walked for hours, reviewing each and every conversation about money that he had engaged in over the past three years. Anything that his brain had filed under *retirement savings* was methodically opened. The files were then duly read aloud by one of two voices: Charles, the conservative planner or the emotional Charlie. The process was painful. At one point, as he neared Chan's Corner Store, he calculated the amount — the actual dollar figure — that he had lost. Charlie had audibly gasped and there was a twinge in his chest.

"Sit down and catch your breath," It was the voice of Charles. "There's a bench near the store where old Mr. Chan holds court every afternoon. Sit there for awhile." He had sat for the better part of an hour. He had thought of all the years he had seen Mr. Chan on this very bench, greeting customers, offering words of wisdom, surveying his life's work while his grandson tended the business. It was a brief distraction that had come to an end, when Charlie tried to reassure his other voice.

"It's not lost unless you sell out," he had repeated Harry's words to Charles. But it had done no good.

"It's only worth what it's worth, not what you hope it'll be." That's how Charles Henderson knew it to be. No surprises. Just the facts. And the fact was, that he had invested a lifetime of saving into mutual funds. From paper boy at age 10 through to the present middle aged mill worker, it was all there. Savings, pension money, all of it...

invested in the unknown world of funds with descriptions like dividend, balanced, income and growth. He'd allowed himself the momentary chuckle at the contradiction between the reality of the markets and the title 'growth equity fund.'

And then the answer came. He knew what needed to be done. Knowledge was power. Charles would do what he knew best. He would change the uncertainty into cold hard facts and reasoning. He would research the history of this enigma that held his money hostage. With facts and figures at hand he would know what to do, how to once again take control of his money and rescue his retirement.

~

"You haven't said a word through lunch. Are you still worried about our retirement money? I tell you Charlie, you'll give yourself a stroke."

"I'm sorry. Look. Don't worry. I'm going to get it all straightened out." He didn't like keeping secrets from Louise. They were not just husband and wife, they were best friends, and he knew it wasn't his money — it was their money — and that made it all the worse. There was no use telling her how much they were down until he knew the answer to her response: 'Well, what do we do now?' Not that she worried about money. Louise cared little about it. Oh, she was careful. She knew every thrift shop within a 50 mile radius, and she never went to Safeway without coupons. But she never made the connection between a required amount of money and retirement.

"When you're ready for retirement you'll retire," she casually stated as if she had been privy to Charles' thoughts. "The money will be there. We'll be fine.... look at my folks."

Lou's folks. Whenever Louise wanted to calm down Charles' money worries, she used the same four words: 'Look at my folks.' There was no arguing. Her folks, now in their eighties, never worried about money.... and yet never did without. Bill Boychuk was a prairie boy, never lived anyplace else. The farm wasn't big enough for three sons and Bill being the youngest made his way to Regina after high school. Twenty odd years later he came back to his home town with two little kids and a pregnant wife. He bought the general store and ran it for thirty years. To hear Bill tell it, he was a huge success.

"Edith and I had saved up most of a thousand dollars. We gave old man Simmonds $800 and he agreed to carry the rest. I was to pay him $100 every month for 15 years. Now you may not think it, but $100 was a lot of money in 1954. There were times when we didn't take out $100 a month for ourselves. But we lived above the store for the first couple of years and we always found something to eat. Every time we had any extra, we put it on the loan. We had Simmonds all paid off three years ahead of schedule. He didn't even keep the last hundred. Turned around and gave it right back. A regular gold mine that store was. Every one in town got supplies there. We raised four kids from that place, not to mention some of the neighbours who couldn't always pay their bills. Then folks started driving to the city for supplies. Why someone would do that, I never could figure out? Drive 70 miles to save $5.00 on a bag of groceries. I was smart enough to get out while the getting was good. Sold out for almost $15,000. That's every penny that I paid for it. Yes sir, that store was a regular gold mine."

Bill and Edith still live in that same town of 300 people, in the same house they bought in 1956 for $1200. Bill told Charlie that he could easily sell it for five times what he paid for it. But they would never sell. When the holidays arrive and the house is full of several generations of Boychuks mixed in with a steady stream of neighbours, you know there is no place more grand than Bill Boychuk's. Charlie would often watch Louise's dad sitting in his Lazy Boy surrounded by those he loved. The big man didn't really fit in the chair. He reminded Charlie of the bread dough he had so often seen in Edith's kitchen, overflowing and spilling out of the stainless steel bowl. When he took his place it was the signal for the grand-kids to scramble for position on the old man's lap. As he watched the clamour and turmoil, interspersed occasionally by Bill's booming laugh, Charlie knew there was no richer man that you could find. When there's a need in the community or a gift to be bought, Edith's purse is the first to open, and you know there is no greater philanthropist. She spoke like a person embarrassed by her affluence.

"Go ahead, Heaven knows we can't spend all we get, what with two Old Age Security cheques and Bill's Canada Pension."

∼

"Charles Henderson were you listening? I usually get at least a grunt."

"Oh I was just thinking about your folks. Just like you told me to do, dear. And you're absolutely right. Your folks are doing just fine. In fact, I can't think of anyone more successful than those two."

"There's no need to get sarcastic."

"No! I mean it. Your dad retired with no more than

his house paid for and a good name. The money he got for the store mostly went to the wholesaler; except for the $4000 he divided amongst you kids. Remember? He said they didn't need it. They would have had more but he wrote off thousands in receivables owed by half the town. And I bet they never give a moment's notice to the latest disaster on Wall and Bay Streets."

"I gather you're still talking about the stock market. Can we think of something else for the weekend? Those mutual funds can't lose anymore money on the weekend, can they?"

"I certainly hope not. But you know me Lou. Once I start thinking about something, it's sort of hard to switch gears. I'm going to do some research this weekend so I know the answers to some questions."

"What research? What questions?"

"Research that I should have done before I got into these funds. Then we'll know what to do. And I can get some sleep."

2

LESSONS FROM
THE MASTERS

"If you want to know what God
thinks about money; just look at
the people he gave it to." ....Dorothy Parker

Charles spent the afternoon at the community
library. He knows it well. It is one of the great treasures in
Victoria. A veritable sanctuary in a commercialize world.
Old men dressed in suits and ties sit in lounge chairs
reading British tabloids about the monarchy. They could
easily be at a gentlemen's private club, but for their fellow
patrons. Within arm's reach one can see youths with
multicoloured hair and painful looking piercings, reading
skate boarding magazines. If there ever was a place that
blurred all boundaries, it is the local library. People from
every segment of society gather with only one factor in
common — the quest for knowledge. There have been
those who prophesied the coming end of libraries with the
proliferation of television and later the dominance of

computers. As Charlie surveyed the room he allowed himself the satisfaction of denouncing another group of false prophets. He had always been amazed that anyone put stock in what the experts had to say. Were they ever right? Charlie was glad that they have been wrong about libraries. Wrong about books. For Charlie is an avid reader of books and as he surveys the crowds he concludes that he is not alone.

There is something about books. A genuineness that can't be found on television. Oh, it is fine to watch the financial market commentators discuss and argue their points of view between commercials for banking services and fast food outlets; but for real research, nothing can beat a book. For here Charles could scrutinize line by line and interrogate the author endlessly. He would begin by looking at the author's background. Why did he write what he did? How do his writings compare with other opinions on the subject? Does his opinion coincide with the facts?

For it was facts that would form the basis of Charles research. He loved numbers. He trusted them. Numbers didn't hide their trueness behind smiles and fancy words. When finance ministers spoke at length in glowing terms of being 'on the road to fiscal responsibility', Charlie and his friends might listen with pleasure, but Charles looked for the numbers. It was all well and good to say the deficit was less than last year but if the bottom line showed a minus it was still a deficit. And if indeed, the country was on the road to recovery, while still spending more than earning, then surely they must be still travelling the wrong way on that road. When CEOs filed reports boasting of increased revenue and market share, Charles look for the numbers. Where were the numbers to show the expenses incurred for the revenue increase? What are the numbers when interest and depreciation are factored in? How are the acquisition costs and stock options being accounted for? What does the balance sheet look like when 'good will' is removed from the asset column? "Show me the numbers."

And now the search was on to find out all he could about this shadowy creature that had his life's savings. What was the stock market? Who controls it? If Charles has lost 30% of his money who, or what, has that 30% now? He learned about the creation of the Dow Jones Index, the bellwether market indicator. And he wrote down the numbers. Each and every year of the Dow's existence and its corresponding performance was recorded. He made notes of world events that might alter the otherwise orderly ebb and flow of the market place. Events like the two world wars, the depression of the thirties, the assassination of world figures and the like. With similar diligence, he followed the trail of inflation and interest rates from the time such things were introduced into man's vocabulary. At ten minutes to eight when the lights were dimmed, signaling the library's imminent closure, Charles was at the check out counter armed with his notebook and an armful of substantial books. He would continue his education at home.

Late into the night Charles read the biographies of the rich. The great names of past generations. How did they master the stock markets? How did they deal with the financial (not to mention emotional) turmoil that is so much a part of equity investing? He carefully considered the lives of John Rockefeller, Andrew Carnegie and J.P Morgan. The early 1800s saw the birth of such legends in the world of industry and high finance. These titans made impressive fortunes in oil and steel and finance. But not in the stock market. At least not in the traditional sense. Not even the financier Morgan, who arranged the mergers and organizing of early corporate America, could be classified as your typical investor. For these moguls were going to the markets for one of two reasons: to attract investors or to buy up public companies and privatize them. And they were not adverse to manipulating the markets to achieve their goals. Such information did nothing to diminish Charles' suspicions.

At the end of the day there were piles of raw data awaiting to be analyzed and conclusions to be drawn. They could wait. He was nearing an answer. The turmoil was abating and Charlie was relaxed enough to sleep.

~

His sleep might have been more peaceful had it not been for Andrew Carnegie, John Rockefeller and Mark Twain. Mark Twain, the alter-ego of Samuel Clements was born in 1835, the same year as Andrew Carnegie. That's where the similarities ended. Before Twain was a famous storyteller and witty philosopher, he was a journalist. So, while Carnegie was ruthlessly amassing a fortune in the steel business, and Rockefeller was making backroom deals with his political cronies to further expand his oil empire, Twain was honing his skills of interviewing the rich and powerful and then...... making fun of them. And so it was that Charlie's sleep, for Charles would not have permitted it, was invaded by the probes of Mark Twain.

To Charlie's astonishment he found himself back in time, inside the hallowed halls of the New York Stock Exchange at number 10 Broad Street, in the presence of these three great men. Mark Twain had convened this gathering for one purpose.

"Mr. Carnegie, Mr. Rockefeller: being as I have known you gentlemen for more years than we will divulge, I decided that you would be the ideal instructors for our friend here, Mr. Charles Henderson. You see, Charles has his savings invested in the stock market and....." Twain paused impatiently before rebuking the two, "There's no call for laughter gentlemen. This is a matter of grave importance. Mr. Henderson would like your advice on saving money for his retirement."

"Please call me Charlie. Charles couldn't make it."

Mr. Rockefeller was the first to speak. "Young man, I made millions in the stock market. It's easy. All you've got to do is start buying up a stock you like, the way I did with The Tidewater Company. You do it real quiet like. If the price is too high why you just start a rumour that their last wild cat hole was a dud. Then you sell a big block of shares and panic the smaller investors. When they're all selling.... you buy. When you own 30 or 40 percent of the shares, you just walk in and take over."

"That's fine JD but I think Charlie here is talking about being one of the smaller investors."

"Look Twain, you can't think small. Or guys like me will murder you. I've told you that a thousand times."

"And don't invest in any company that's got union workers," It was the voice of Andrew Carnegie. "Those radicals are trying to ruin me at Homestead."

"Maybe the workers are looking for a better deal, Andy."

"Don't start with me, Mark. The men get ten dollars a week and every July 4th off. Nobody's holding a

Winchester to their head. There's plenty of other folks that
will work for that pay. Besides, life is more than money. I
have known millionaires starving for lack of the nutrients
which alone can sustain all that is human in man, and I
know workmen, and many so-called poor men, who revel in
luxuries beyond the power of those millionaires to reach.
There is no class so pitiably wretched as that which
possesses money and nothing else."

"Well said Mr. Carnegie. Did I write that?" Twain
teased.

"My good man. You know that I too am a man of
letters. I have published articles as have you."

"But mine are original. I believe you borrowed one
of your best sayings from me. 'Put all your eggs in one
basket. Then watch that basket.'"

Charlie interrupted. "Boy, things sure have changed
since 1895. Now the financial planners are telling us to
diversify, don't have all your eggs in one basket."

"Who in blazes is a financial planner? Whoever he
is, I'll wager he doesn't have a basket as big as mine."
Carnegie boasted.

"A financial planner is someone who knows all
about money, and investing, and planning for retirement."
Charlie explained.

"So he's rich like Andrew and me?" Mr Rockefeller
queried.

"No. Not that rich. He tells other people how to get
rich."

"Sounds like your old man JD," Twain interjected.
"Only he used to travel around selling elixir to cure all your
aches and pains. That man could sell a Bible to the Devil
himself."

"Did we come here to talk about my Daddy or to help this fellow? Look here. If you're going to invest and make money you've got to get big, like I said. And you need an angle — a little advantage over everyone else. Like Andy here. He was working for Scott who was a boss of the Pennsylvania Railroad. So he finds out that they're about to buy sleeper cars from Woodruff. So naturally, he buys shares in Woodruff Sleeping Car Company."

"I made a fortune," Mr. Carnegie voices in agreement.

"Uh... you can't do that now. It's called insider trading and it's illegal," Charlie begins to explain. "You see it's like this...."

"I didn't say it was LEGAL!" Rockefeller roars. "I said it was PROFITABLE! The legal stuff is for the lawyers. They talk to the judges and politicians. You make a deal and everybody's happy. You set up a charity and build a library or give a bunch of organs to some churches."

"And you invest in a company that has no competition," Carnegie adds. "I control 80% of the steel manufacturing and JD controls over 90% of the oil. We either bought out the competition or forced them out of business. With no competition you buy from suppliers at your price and you sell to customers at your price."

"But, but...." He held his tongue. Charlie knew it was futile to continue with anything as mundane as competition laws and morals. Instead he turns to his host, Mark Twain. "And you Mr. Twain, are you a successful investor?"

Now Charlie had read the accounts of Carnegie and Rockefeller. Their biographers had described them as men who publicly showed little emotion. They were wrong. At the mere mention of Mark Twain's investing acumen, the two industrialists collapsed into giggles associated with school children. In vivid detail and with unsuppressed laughter they chronicled one investment after another in which Twain had ventured, only to lose all his capital. They told how he had invested heavily into mining stocks as they flirted with the promise to revisit the boom times during the gold rush of `49.

Twain winced as the story was told. It may have been years since he had lost his investment, but the pain was still there. Charlie knew just how he felt. Twain's response was typical for a writer. He blended his loss into the big picture of greed and dishonesty, proclaiming:

"That quest for gold in California was the watershed event that sanctified a new money worship and debased the country's founding ideals."

"Money worship" indeed. What would the author of Tom Sawyer think of Charlie's world?

The record of his investment decisions continued. He was a famous author and naturally wanted to be a publisher. Disaster. He frequently financed inventors but in return only got another humourous story for the telling. There seemed to be no end to the trail of Twain's losses.

"One last question Charlie, for our two distinguished instructors?" Twain was trying to wind the session to a close before Rockefeller and Carnegie decided to relate some more stories that he would like to forget.

Charlie pondered. One last question that would aid him in his financial decisions. One truism, one spark of wisdom that would act as a beacon as he groped for a secure happy retirement. When the question surfaced it was obvious. There could be no other question.

"Are you happy? You gentlemen have acquired tremendous financial wealth and power. Now as you near retirement, are you happy?"

John Rockefeller was first off the mark. "What's happiness got to do with it? Look Charlie, don't let a search for happiness or good fellowship get hold of you or you'll never be rich."

Andrew Carnegie differed with his colleague. He spoke not as a conquering tycoon but with the disappointment of a man who had gambled and lost. "Don't envy me, young man. I'm 60 years old and cannot digest my food. I would give all my millions if I could have youth and health. I would gladly sell anything to have my life over again."

3

EASY CREDIT

"I can get no remedy against this consumption
of the purse: borrowing only lingers and lingers
it out, but the disease is incurable." ..Henry IV, Act 1

Charles was behind his schedule. To begin his week-long vacation behind schedule was a major setback. His plans would need to change. And that could only be bad. It heralded uncertainty; and Charles hated uncertainty.

"As soon as we get on board the ferry, we must call Ken and let him know we will be late. Really Louise, I don't know why you let me sleep in. You know I hate changing plans."

"Calm down. It's not the end of the world. You were thrashing around so much in the night I just knew you would be tired. It's only a couple of hours. We'll still be at their place in plenty of time."

"It wouldn't be so bad if it wasn't for this rotten ferry. Two and half hours to go 24 miles. That's once we get going. The worst part is sitting here waiting. I don't know why we isolate ourselves on the island?"

"Yes you do. It's because it's isolated. We moved here thirty years ago because you wanted to get away from all my relatives. Remember? And every time we make the crossing you carry on about the ferry. I quite enjoy it, and you would too if you didn't enjoy complaining even more."

The traffic director signaled for them to join the slow procession of vehicles as they snaked their way from the parking lot to an overpass and across the ramp into the belly of the *Queen of Alberni*. Charlie wedged their 10 year old Volvo wagon into place and shut off the motor. The car was an extension of Charles, predictable, conservative, very little risk. He had bought it as a lease return seven years ago. He never gave any thought to upgrading — not like so many of the fellows at the mill who trade every two years. What kind of financial plan is that? You wouldn't catch Warren Buffett wasting money like that.

Louise opened her door to exit. Charlie sat and waited. He had watched in his side mirror as the aging Chevy pick-up with the oversized tires pulled tightly along side. The passenger, who might have been a sumo wrestler in another part of the world, was attempting to exit. The Volvo rocked with the impact of the truck's door. Charlie found himself counting the number of blows inflicted on his old friend. It was useless to say anything. "It only adds to the makings of a memorable trip," he thought. He caught up to Louise on the stairs to the lounge area, and continued his complaining.

"They'll be waiting supper for us. I hate that. It's five hours to Kamloops after we dock at Tswassen. That'll put us there at eight o'clock. What time is that to eat supper?"

"It's a perfectly splendid time to eat supper. You've said so yourself a hundred times. Now look here Charles Henderson, I know you're tired and still worried about that stupid retirement plan of yours. But if you think you are going to ruin this trip for me, forget it. I'm going to have a fun time with my family if it kills you."

When Louise called her husband *Charles Henderson* he knew he had crossed the line. It was fine to rant and rave to a point, but just so far. It was time to make a hasty retreat.

"Yeah you're right. I'm just being difficult again. We'll call your nephew and then I'll treat you to lunch. Maybe I'll catch an hour's sleep on the way across the strait."

"I'll call. You go get in line. I will be back before you reach the order counter. I'll need your card for the pay phone." Louise had packed a lunch but it would do Charlie good to eat the ferry food. She smiled and whispered to herself as she reached for the phone. "It'll give him something different to complain about."

~

It wouldn't be a long visit at Ken and Marie's. It was just an overnight stop. Their real destination was Golden Prairie — the village where Louise's folks lived. It was a two-day drive from the island to Louise's folks. When Charlie and Louise were first married, after the best impressions had worn thin, Charlie and his in-laws ..... well it was a awkward relationship — at best. Charlie, or at least Charles, was pretty definite in his ways and he didn't mind saying so. The Boychuks were family people, so many relatives and they were always underfoot. There was never a minute's privacy. And so much advice. Louise never noticed all the commotion but Charles had been raised differently. He was an only child and he was used to being alone. He enjoyed it. He demanded it. His solution was to move. Yes it was a good two-day drive, a marvelous two-day drive.

That was thirty years ago. Over the years as they made a life for themselves, he came to appreciate the values that the Boychuks had passed on to their daughter. Louise had many qualities that Charlie admired. While he was tense in a crowd, she was at ease. She didn't understand Charles' aversion to social gatherings, nor did Charlie, but it was Louise that made the excuses for why they couldn't accept yet another invitation. Louise was a people person, genuinely interested in everyone, regardless of their background or economic standing in the community. She was the first to offer help to a neighbour, the first to make a hospital visit with a card and flowers, or see a need that Charlie was oblivious to. Just like her mom. She didn't bother to have Charles sign the card. He would only flip it over and make a face when he saw the price. And when disputes arose with friends or neighbours, as they invariable did, it was Louise who set things right. Just like her dad. She never insisted that Charlie change but change he had. Well he wasn't a Boychuk, but he had drifted a short distance in that direction.

The thing that had annoyed Charles the most was the way the Boychuks handled money — or mishandled it without careful planning for the future. He had cast dire predictions for their old age; "We will end up looking after them." He had warned Louise. The thought haunted Charles but Louise had warmly smiled and said she looked forward to that day.

But he had been wrong. The experts with their graphs on inflation and the $60-a-barrel oil and $2000 gold had been wrong. Charles had ceased making predictions and hoped everyone had forgotten his warnings. Not that they had given his words much weight. Oh, they had politely listened, and Edith would say how clever he was with numbers and statistics and such, but for all his efforts to get their financial house in order they had never changed. And here they were. Hale and hearty, well into their eighties and living as comfortably as any couple Charlie knew.

Now Charlie and his in-laws were close friends. He looked forward to the annual trip over the March break. He listened with a new respect to Bill's stories. He heard himself repeating some of Bill's favourite sayings. "I never would've thought I'd be happy to see all those Boychuks. It's amazing how much Louise's folks have changed over the years," Charlie chuckled as he drove the last few miles to Kamloops.

Kenny is Louise's nephew. He and his wife Marie live in Kamloops. It's a good stop-over spot on the way to Louise's folks. They've made the stop for the past five trips but this will be the first time to see the new house. Louise has promised Wilma, her sister and Kenny's mom, that they would look in on the young couple. Kenny's folks have been worried about them. They haven't heard much from them lately. To a parent that can only mean there must be something to worry over.

"This is a beautiful view looking over the city and the Thompson," Louise comments as they wind their way up the street leading to Ken and Marie's. It's a new subdivision. Most of the snow has melted exposing the manicured lawns and cultured shrubbery as neighbours compete in replicating English gardens.

"There it is," Louise says while gesturing to the appropriate driveway.

Charlie pulls in alongside a late model Yukon.

"I think your sister's got herself worked up about nothing. It looks to me like Ken and Marie are doing just fine. I hope there's still some supper left. I didn't eat much of the lunch we got on the ferry."

Ken and Marie have seen them pull in and are standing at the entrance. Ken has the twins hoisted in each arm. A picture of the consummate suburban family.

"I just love your house!" Louise exclaims as they are ushered in through the foyer, past the family room, and into the dining area.

Ken follows Charlie's eyes as he appraises the rooms they pass. He doesn't wait for Charlie to speak.

"We haven't got around to furnishing all the rooms yet. It's much bigger than our last place. We just put some of these old things in for now. They'll all be replaced eventually."

The couples exchange looks and the topic is changed to centre on supper and how much the children have grown. When the table has been cleared and the twins are sound asleep, Marie returns to the inevitable.

"To tell you the truth Louise, we're broke."

"We don't want any money from family," Ken quickly adds, "but we could use some advice. Do you have any suggestions for us? We'd like to get our costs of living down so that we have a little more family time. I feel guilty that I have so little time with the kids. I'm either working or just too tired to give them the attention they deserve."

"And it's not just the kids. We see each other even

less," Marie joins in. "Ken gets home from work at 5:30 and I start work at 7:00. Ken works 5 days a week and I work 6 evenings a week. Today's the only day you'd catch us together.

"That's a lot of hours working. Do you really need to work that much?" Louise queries.

"We do if we want to hold on to the house. When we bought it last year I was working on the pipeline. Then I got laid off, and with my new job I'm making less than half the money. Marie took on extra work just to pay some bills."

"How much do you need to make to keep all the balls in the air?" Charlie asks.

"We added up our payments and they come to almost $2600. And then there's food and clothes and kids' stuff. We need over $4500 before all the deductions," Marie is reciting from a memorized list. "And that's $200 more than we earn with us both working all the time."

"Are you sure your payments are that high? I had no idea that it was so expensive to own a house in Kamloops."

"Well Charlie, it's not just the house," Ken explains. "The house is $1400 and my truck is another $550. Then there's a bank loan and the minimum payment on our credit cards."

"Can't you sell the house and get out from under this debt?" Charlie's anxiety level is rising.

"Calm down Charlie. It's not your problem," Charles reminds him.

"We had our house appraised and it's not worth any more than we paid for it. Any realtor fees would eat away the little equity that we have in the house... that's if we could sell it. I'm not the only guy who has been laid off from the oil patch."

"And the truck?" Louise ventures.

"But I need my truck. I need something to get me to work."

"But not that truck, Kenny. A cheaper truck would do just as well," Marie speaks as if this subject has been talked about before.

Louise and Charlie decided to call it a night. Charles had more to add but for once Charlie was in control. Getting rid of the $550 per month truck is the start. If Ken and Marie are serious — really serious — about getting their life back, they will need to do more. The house will have to go. Even if they come away with no cash, they're better off. They can rent for less. Building equity should not be a priority. If they don't sell the house they'll lose it to the bank soon enough. Yes dump that fancy truck and sell the house. Conserving money is the goal.

"You should have let me say something. I was just going to tell them how to get their life in order, Charlie."

"They know what to do Charles. The question is: Will they do it?"

~

Both couples were up before dawn. Marie was making Ken's breakfast while Ken was fixing sandwiches for lunch.

"Don't make anything for us," Louise called out between trips to the car. "We like to drive for a bit before breakfast. We'll stop at Salmon Arm."

"I can't wait to get on the road," Charlie said as Kamloops faded in the rear view mirror. "Those kids are in a real bind. It's depressing thinking about it. Why do people get in over their heads like that?"

"Because they can, Charlie. It's too easy to borrow

money. Just look at all the credit card applications that we get in the mail; pre-approved for thousands of dollars. It's easy getting in. It's the getting out that will take some doing."

"Well it's out of our hands. Where should we stop in Salmon Arm for breakfast? There's a Smitty's on the highway. It must be your turn to buy." The words were only partly in jest. "I saw a fifty in your pocketbook yesterday. Don't be holding out on me Lou."

"Look again Charlie," as she flashed her opened wallet. "That was yesterday. The fifty's stuck inside a thank you card at Ken and Marie's."

"Aww! What did you go and do that for? We're not made of money."

"Don't be so cheap. Fifty dollars is a pretty good price for a motel room in Kamloops. And besides we aren't suffering. And even if we were, it feels good to give. You should try it Charlie! Ken and Marie can use a little help right now. That little bit won't solve any of their money problems but maybe they'll buy something with it and it'll remind them that we are thinking of them. That's what WE wrote in the card dear."

"All right. I was gonna get breakfast anyway. That was nice of you to leave the money. But next time can you do it with a twenty?"

By the time they sat down at Smitty's it was eight o'clock. They'd been on the road for an hour and a half. Charlie was famished and settled into the *farmer's breakfast*. Louise sat calmly sipping on a cup of Earl Grey and eating a slice of whole grain toast — lightly buttered. When she finished she casually pulled out her Weight Watcher's calorie counter and started adding up the points.

"Come on Lou, we're on vacation," he protested. "Besides I will exercise and wear off the extra points."

"Charlie, with what you've eaten you'd have to jog to Revelstoke to wear it off. Just don't make any sudden moves or those pants are history."

By eight forty-five they were back on the road. Charlie loved the drive through the Shuswap and into the Rockies. They'd travelled the same highway annually for close to thirty years but it was always fresh. In the early morning the mist hung over the lakes like a stage curtain awaiting the arrival of all the actors. If the sky was clear, the sun would make a timid appearance among the treetops or perhaps slowly rise behind a summit. Today was such a day. Not a cloud in the sky. By the time they reached the first range of hills, the mist was gone. The roads were clear but there was still plenty of snow in the woods and on the hills. Charlie needed his sunglasses to ward off the glare. You never knew what to expect driving through the mountains in late March. One minute you are reaching for sunglasses and the next you need a shovel and chains. Of course they were prepared. Charles wouldn't take any risks. Stored in the Volvo next to a folding shovel and the tire chains were sleeping bags, a portable radio, a small axe, flashlight with extra batteries, flares, matches, compass, candles, and enough chocolate to ruin a lifetime of dieting.

They stopped on the way out of Golden to watch a flock of mountain sheep that had come down from the cliffs looking for some early grass that had been coaxed out of the sod by the warm spring sun. It was noon. They would be at the Boychuks' for supper. The Boychuks knew all about eating late. It was as if they were always waiting for someone else to show up for supper. Charlie couldn't recall being there when there wasn't extra places set. Yes they'd be there by eight. There was time to stop and watch.

There were three ewes and a couple of yearlings. The ram wasn't in sight. Charlie wondered if it was close to lambing and the ram was off on his own. He liked to watch wildlife. He could draw valuable lessons from them.

"I bet they're not worried about retirement."

"Who's not worried?" Louise said, as she looked someone that Charlie might be referring to.

"They... them, the sheep. Look at them Louise. Not a care in the world. Just enjoying the moment. We could learn from them you know."

"You could learn from them Charlie. I'm not worried about retirement. I've been telling you that for years. Go ahead. Listen to what they tell you. At least listen to one of us."

"Of course the male's not there," Charlie began with a smirk. "He's probably gone to buy some mutual funds."

"Another dumb animal!" Louise sniped.

"Ouch. Time to go. I've got to stop leading with my chin. You're getting all the good lines, Louise."

4

BARGAINS - SUPPLY & DEMAND

"Necessity never made
a good bargain." .... Poor Richard (1758)

The sunglasses remained in their case when Charlie resumed driving. Clouds had moved in from the east. An hour later the first flakes of snow were skimming past the windshield. He turned on the radio for the forecast. They were in the middle of the Rockies, a no-man's zone when it comes to radio reception. There was no signal. Another half hour and they passed the Banff turn-off. Two summers ago they had opted for a late lunch in Banff. It had been a mistake. The sidewalks were jostling with people. It might have been Toronto or Vancouver. Charlie couldn't understand the attraction of driving for hours to a wilderness area only to be surrounded by the masses. And the prices. It would have been cheaper in Toronto and easier to find a parking spot.

But he loved the mountains, the majesty of towering

snow capped peaks that dominated life below. A century earlier
the architect of the Banff Hotel had captured that rugged
permanence. It joined the mountains in overshadowing
everything in the town. He had even inquired about staying. The
desk clerk had smiled condescendingly when Charles inquired
about availability.

"Do we have rooms available, with no reservation, in the
middle of July?" He paraphrased Charles request with sufficient
volume to alert the throngs congregated in the lobby that here
was a peasant who had no business being in such an
establishment. "We are fully booked for the months of July and
August until 2005. And no sir I'm afraid we do not... *dicker* —
as you say — over the price of accommodation. Perhaps if you
would try the Motel 6 in Canmore they would have something
more suitable to your standards."

No, they had no desire to stop at Banff today.

And besides it was snowing. Snowing in earnest. The
road was covered and Charles took over the wheel from Charlie.
He reduced his speed — then second guessed his decision. It
appeared as if he was the only one who had noticed the snow.
Other cars were gliding past, even semis with their headlights
flashing, telling him to speed up or get out of the way.

He reached to take off his sunglasses and then
remembered they weren't on. As they passed the exit for
Canmore he could see the service stations all lit up in the dusk.
He looked at the clock in the dash. It was just after three. Ten
kilometers past Canmore there was the first of many vehicles in
the ditch. The Town Car that had passed them moments earlier
was now motionless, half buried in snow while the driver and
passenger scrambled up the embankment into the waiting car of
a Good Samaritan. Charles reduced his speed some more.

"It's getting worse the farther we drive. We're still a

half hour out of Calgary. A half hour in good driving. I wonder what the forecast is?" He spoke more to himself than to Louise as he turned on the radio and hit the search button.

"Batten down the hatches folks. We're in for a late winter's storm and this one looks like a doosey!" came the reply to Charlie's question from the announcer on QR77. He continued with a list of cancellations of community events and then the words Charles dreaded. "The RCMP are warning motorists to stay off the roads."

"What should we do Charlie?"

"There's nothing that we can do but keep driving. There's no sense in going back to Canmore. We can't get off this freeway even if we wanted to. We'll just stay behind this trucker — if I can catch him — and hope he stays on the road."

By the time they crawled to the city limits it was five o'clock and the city of Calgary was shut down. All the plows had been pulled off except for hospital routes and the Trans Canada which runs through the city disguised as 16th. There was no traffic east of Calgary. The number 2 to Lethbridge was blocked with snow and the Trans Canada had a jack-knifed semi blocking both lanes.

"I'd better call my folks. They'll be worried sick. Where's the cell phone?"

Charles' eyes remained focused on the road. He pointed to the glove compartment. He wasn't a big fan of having the latest technology but he was a believer in the cellular phone. It had come in handy on many occasions. It was one bill that he paid without much grumbling. Unfortunately everyone else on the face of the earth thought it was a good idea too. When you add a situation like a major snowfall the result is predictable.

"I can't get through. The circuits are all busy."

"We'll call from a motel."

"What motel?"

"Any motel. The first one we come to."

The first one was the Sheraton near the Olympic ski jump. They had splurged and stayed there just after the winter games in `98. The crowds had gone and the motel had been deserted. It had been the perfect time to rent a room. Charlie remembered the hagglng like it was yesterday. In the end he had a $145 room for $69. The night manager had eagerly agreed to the price. Too eager. Charlie had offered too much. Charles would have done better. He would do better tonight.

"I'd like a room for the night. Two people. What's the rate?"

"A superior room for two people. A very nice room with one king size bed for $189."

"No, no." Charles began the negotiations. "Not for the week. Just one night. Look Raj — it is Raj?" he paused waiting for the nod to confirm the name on the tag of the desk clerk. He was young. Perhaps there would be a need to speak to someone with more authority to reduce the rate.

"Raj, look outside," he continued, "the roads are closed. There is no one else showing up tonight. The rooms will be empty. Why not take a little less — say.... half — and we're both happy. Is there a manager here that could make that decision?"

"I'm sorry sir, but that is the rate. And it is the *last* room available." The words were still on the edge of the desk clerk's lips when Charles heard a voice over his shoulder.

"I'll take it! Here's my American Express."

Charles turned as the traveller did a head fake and dipsy doodled around him. It was a classic deke that would have any hockey fan on his feet, cheering. He was by Charles in a flash and taking possession of the space in front of the counter and the last room at the Sheraton.

And the last hotel room in Calgary — a fact not lost on the traveller as he clutched his room key on the way to the elevator.

It had been snowing in Calgary since noon. By four most of the businesses had given up and closed their doors sending employees skidding home. When the arteries out of town were closed, motorists made a quick rush for the motels.

There was to be no bargains tonight.

~

"Ladies and gentlemen. Welcome to Calgary International Airport. Please remain seated until the aircraft has come to a complete stop and the captain has switched off the seat belt sign. For passengers continuing to Victoria, Saskatoon or Edmonton, please contact the Air Canada ticket counter. For passengers who will be terminating their flight in Calgary, have a good evening. On behalf of Captain Rogers and all the crew we would like to thank you for flying with Air Canada and look forward to seeing you again soon."

Michael Tibbet was not concerned. He was on his way back to Victoria but he was in no great hurry. His hurrying days were behind him now that he was retired. A little delay due to the weather, he thought. The captain had commented on the snow when they began their flight in Mazatlan. There had been the expected groans from vacationers reminded of Canadian weather. This was March and a little snow was nothing unusual for Calgary.

He waited for most of the passengers to disembark. When the aisle was clear he stood up, reached for his carry-on and made his way off the aircraft and toward the Air

Canada ticket counter. He wasn't alone. There were long line-ups and animated conversations with the beleaguered ticket agents. The bits of dialogue that Michael overheard suggested there would be more than a little delay. Long before he reached the counter the announcement confirmed the rumours.

"For the interest of all departing passengers. Due to the weather and runway conditions, all outgoing flights have been cancelled until further notice. Please check with the respective carriers for further instructions. For those awaiting incoming flights please check for any arrival changes."

~

"It's been a while since I stayed in Calgary." Michael said to the driver, as he surveyed the rest of the passengers being shuttled to the Bow River Manor. Seven in all.

There was Tom Fisher and his wife Florence, both in their sixties. They lived outside of Saskatoon on the same farm his grandfather homesteaded before Saskatchewan entered Confederation. Tom was wearing bright walking shorts and the complimentary T-shirt that informed everyone that you had stayed in Vegas and had a wonderful time. They were never made for middle aged men who enjoyed their food and an occasional beer. He would have felt more comfortable in coveralls but Florence had vetoed his choice of apparel.

The shuttle bus had waited while Tammy and Rick Clarke, with Jessica and Tyler in tow, re-packed their luggage and scrambled on board. Immigration had taken an unusual interest in the young family. They were returning to Hanna, a small town east of Red Deer, after six months in the Dominican Republic. Five year old Tyler hardly resembled the picture on his identification. In addition to his dark skin his speech was peppered with *Hola* and *Esta bien.*

～

Charlie prevailed upon the desk clerk to phone every establishment in the city. Perhaps there was a cancellation, a sudden illness or death that would leave a room vacant. Remove the body and Charlie would pay whatever they asked.

Raj began making inquiries from a list. One after another he made the calls. Each time the scene was replayed. There was the brief introduction, a request for any available rooms, followed by an upward glance and a somber shaking of his head in Charlie's direction. Sometimes the conversation ended with Raj laughing and speaking quickly in his mother tongue — perhaps Punjabi. Charles was sure he was the object of ridicule. Louise had tired of waiting in the car and came in to make inquiries of her own. She had taken a chair in the lobby. Charles made no mention of his previous negotiating tactics.

Twenty minutes into the search, the desk clerk motioned for Charles' attention.

"Mr. Henderson, Sir, I have secured accommodations for you."

"Excellent. You're a good man, Raj. This is for your trouble," He dug under several twenties and pulled out a five, presenting it to his benefactor. "Now how do we find this hotel? I'll need a city map."

"Here it is." Raj was circling the street on a map. "So we are here and you need to take the highway to the Sarcee Trail turn-off. Turn left on 25th Avenue and follow it about one kilometer. It is a big house on the right, number 1171," He was drawing a line along the route with a red marker.

"A house, you booked us a house for the night?"

"Not the whole house, Mr. Henderson. A room in the house. It is a very nice old house. It is called Bow River Manor, a bed and breakfast establishment. It is owned and operated by Mr. and Mrs. Daliwahl. You should tell them that Raj sent you."

"I'm right behind you dear," Louise called as Charlie sprinted for the car. In the forty-five minutes they had been in the hotel, several more inches of snow had piled up on the roof of the car. While Charlie was brushing off the car, Louise approached the desk clerk.

"Thank you for all your help. This is for you." and she handed him a twenty. "My husband is just learning this giving thing and he hasn't quite got the hang of it yet. I'm Louise Henderson."

"Thank you Mrs. Henderson. And I am Raj. Raj Daliwahl.

~

The trip to the house on 25th was uneventful, if slow is not an event. For living on Vancouver Island all his life, Charles was a good winter driver. And of course the new snow tires that he had bought for the trip were proving to be a good investment. Before leaving the Sheraton, he had considered installing the chains but after a brief conversation with Charlie, he had withdrawn the suggestion. It hadn't been necessary. He followed a snow-plow all the way to 25th. The house numbers were obscured by the falling snow but he pulled into the obvious driveway. It was the only one cleared of snow. The snow blower was still working around the back, finishing the parking lot. There were two other vehicles. One must belong to the owners of the inn. The K car gave evidence that its owner was not a recent guest. It was buried under snow. Charles parked beside it. As they emerged from the Volvo, the operator of the blower shut it down and came over.

"I am Bibi Daliwahl, your host. Please let me help you with your things."

"Charles...uh Charlie Henderson and this is Louise. A bit of a wasted effort clearing the lot don't you think?"

"We are expecting more guests. It is my job to get you in. Once you are here it may take longer for you to get out. That Mr. Henderson, will be your job." Bibi followed his comments with laughter. Charles made an effort to join in the joke but his pained grin displayed the fear that perhaps there was no joke.

The house dated back to the beginning of the 1900s. Prior to World War 1 when the world was civilized and life was a quiet evening spent in front of a fire with good food and the best of friends. The stonework and intricate detail on the gables was the signature of craftsmen whose work spoke eloquently of the time and skill dedicated to the house in equal measure.

"Hello. I'm Elizabeth Daliwahl." The lady of the manor was at the front door extending her hand as they approached. She paused before continuing. She was always quick to introduce herself. It took strangers a moment to get used to the idea of a fair skinned woman with a faint British accent having a surname from the Punjab. Thirty-five years ago when they had married in Brighton, outside London, there had been no shortage of gossip. But this was 2003 and in Canada — *The New World* — where these things were acknowledged if not totally accepted. Still, an early introduction saved any explanation as to her role.

"What a dreadful evening. I am so happy you arrived safely. Here. Come in. Come in. Bibi, see if you can find some slippers. No. Why don't you show our friends to their room and I'll get the slippers."

As Mrs. Daliwahl scurried off, Louise slipped off her boots. She nudged Charlie to do the same. The highly polished oak floors dictated that footwear be removed. "The place is beautiful." she said as much to Charlie as to Bibi who was leading them up the formal staircase.

"Thank you Mrs. Henderson."

"You really must call me Louise."

"Yes. And Charlie for me. Have you had this house for long?"

"We have lived here for over twenty years. We raised our three children here. When the children moved out we decided to make it into a Bed and Breakfast. You will be in Margaret's room. She is our youngest."

"Margaret?"

"Yes. Our two girls, Margaret and Priscilla, were named by my wife. I picked the name for our son — Raj. I believe you have met him?"

Bibi opened the bedroom door and Louise followed him inside. Charlie was still in the hall. He had stopped in surprise with the mention of Raj. He had expected his wife to be as surprised as he at this relationship between the desk clerk and their current host. But there it was. That small smile that gave her away. She had known all along — again. He shook his head softly and returned her smile.

The room was definitely feminine, fuchsias and teals with lace curtains and porcelain dolls displayed throughout. The original design of the room had never been altered. There was no closet; but a large mahogany wardrobe that stood serenely on guard. And the dressing chest complete with secret trays that in the recent past hid precious jewelry and diaries of teenage girls.

"The room looks like a Priscilla," Louise remarked in a low voice more to herself than to contradict her guide.

"Indeed it is," confirmed Elizabeth as she entered bearing two pairs of lamb skin slippers. "Bibi you haven't forgotten which of the girls had this room? Pris has only been away for less than a year."

"You're more likely to find dissected frogs and skeletons in the wardrobe next door in Peggy's room. She's a vet working in Red Deer. Is this room suitable for you folks?"

"It's wonderful."

"How much?" Charles was back.

"Make a deal with Bibi," Elizabeth suggested. "We aren't officially open. We only returned from England two days ago. Raj called and said the city's full of stranded travellers and could we help. We don't usually begin our season until the first of May."

"Our rate is in the brochure on the night stand," added Bibi. "but Charlie, you set the price. Before you leave and after you've had Bess's biscuits in the morning."

"And after I've shovelled out the car."

"Before you've shovelled out the car." There was the laughter of four old friends in the room.

Their hosts left them to settle into their room. Louise tried to reach her folks again. On the third attempt she got through and relayed the reason for their delay and assurances that they were comfortable for the night.

"We'll see you tomorrow. Don't worry about supper. It'll keep. We'll have it for lunch. We're fine mom. Yes we'll get something to eat. Tell dad not to shovel the walk. Charlie will be happy to do it when we get there."

"I'm 53 years old and mom still worries that I won't eat

enough supper." Louise was shaking her head as she hung-up. "Of course I'd be disappointed if she ever stopped."

"Speaking of supper, What are the odds of us finding something to eat tonight? I'm going to need my strength for tomorrow. Between you and our host here, you've lined up a lot of snow shovelling for me."

"There's a bag in the car with some nuts and a couple of apples in it. That'll have to do. There won't be anything open, even if we could get out of the parking lot."

Charlie retrieved the bag from the car. Several more inches of snow had fallen. Louise was right. No one in his right mind would venture out tonight. The thought of missing supper only made Charlie hungrier. He remembered the chocolate stored away with the other emergency supplies. He hadn't eaten in seven hours. Would that be considered an emergency? He looked up and saw Louise in their bedroom window. She was watching. The chocolate was safe in the car — for now.

As Charlie headed back to his room Bibi appeared in the hallway. "Charlie. You and Mrs. Henderson must come down and join us. I have started a fire and it is more comfortable here. Please come."

"Thank you. I'll tell Louise and we'll be down in a moment." Charlie answered from the top of the stairs. "After I've eaten everything in this bag," he whispered to himself as he entered the bedroom.

5

FAMILY MATTERS

"He is happiest, be he king
or peasant, who finds peace
in his home."....Johann Von Goethe

It surely was more comfortable downstairs in the parlour. Bibi was sitting close to the fireplace where he could nourish the flames with an ample supply of dried maple. The fireplace was the focal point of the room with a variety of couches and armchairs positioned in a semi-circle before it. The walls were panelled in dark veneers sought after by the well-to-do at the beginning of the nineteen hundreds. They were brightened by the paintings of the English countryside and ancient castles. One wall housed a tantalizing collection of books. Louise pictured herself curled up in the leather loveseat engrossed in the adventures of Inspecteur Perrault. Charles wondered if there might be anything about Andrew Carnegie.

"Louise. Sit here near the fire," Bibi gestured to the chair that he was abandoning. "There are more guests arriving and I must make sure that the walk is clear. But first you must meet my cousin Badra and his two beautiful daughters. They have been staying here looking after the manor while we've been away. Badra lives in Vancouver, so you are neighbours." Charlie and Louise hadn't noticed anyone else in the room. Badra and his girls had been sitting in one of the couches away from the fire, in the shadows. As Bibi introduced them, they rose and greeted the Hendersons.

"Oh, I hope we haven't taken over one of your bedrooms," Louise voiced her sudden concern, remembering that the Manor had not been expecting guests."

"No problem," Badra assured Louise. "There is a lovely suite in the attic that we are using. It is bigger than my place in Vancouver."

"Are you staying here much longer? When do you head back to Vancouver?" Charlie quizzed.

"My daughters live in Calgary — with their mother. They are all grown up. Ranjna is 24 and Rabetta is 18. I will go back as soon as the roads are clear. And you Charlie, are you on your way back to the island?"

"No. We are headed to Saskatchewan to see Lou's folks and whoever else of her family shows up."

"Family. You are a wealthy man Mr. Henderson!"

"Not even close, Badra. Don't get me started about my investments."

"*Please don't,* Badra," pleaded Louise.

"Charlie Henderson. When I speak of wealth I am not talking about stocks and bonds or bank accounts. I have had all of those and was poor. Now I live in a small trailer, but I have an abundance. Here is my wealth." Badra puts his arms around his daughters and draws them close.

"Ranjna, Rabetta, may we tell our new friends our story? Perhaps someone else may learn from it."

The children nod in approval and Badra begins:

"I live in a small two bedroom trailer in a mobile home park on the outskirts Vancouver. Many have less," he ponders; "It is better than the east end where I lived for awhile."

The east end — one of the poorest places, in one of the richest cities, in Canada. An area where the displaced and disoriented come to mingle with purveyors of misery and pain. An area where reporters converge upon all too frequently to chronicle the latest homicide. Where television cameras callously record the plight of lives picked over by the masses and discarded as unsuitable. An area where the reporters and cameras quickly retreat to more comfortable surroundings; free from the needles, condoms, blood and urine.

And seven miles from the east side is the residence that he once shared with his family. Seven miles, but a world apart. In West Van the world is a place of privilege and opportunity. A place of private schools and nannies and grounds keepers. A place where Badra felt at home among his peers. But that is in the past. A past that Badra and his girls share with the Hendersons.

"I immigrated to Canada over twenty years ago, with my wife Sadheep, and Ranjna. Rabetta was born in this country, she is a Canadian," he adds with a degree of pride.

"Our parents helped us. It was 'for a better life'. Sadheep was a teacher. I have a degree in engineering from India and I had a good position there, but we had heard of the opportunities in Canada. I quickly got work. I was a bus-boy at a very nice restaurant — The Chan Dynasty — for two years. Then I became a waiter. My wife got a job with one of the engineering firms in the city. She was cleaning the offices, the lobby, the washrooms." Badra pauses allowing the irony to register. "Sometimes she would be asked to clean the homes of the executives. Sadheep would come back to our small apartment and tell me about the fine homes. When the children were sleeping, we would hold hands and speak softly about the future, as young lovers do. I would promise that one day we would have such a fine house. I can still feel her hands. They were coarse and shriveled from the scrubbing and cleansers. She smelled of bleach and soap. I would tell her that soon she would have housekeepers and Ranjna and Rabetta would not have to stay with my cousin when we worked.

"We were miserly with our money. After eight years we had saved twenty thousand dollars. We started our own computer design company. Every spare hour, after our regular jobs, was devoted to our new enterprise — Manhas Networks. It was at the perfect time. So many businesses were scrambling to introduce computers to their operations. After a year of working from our kitchen table, and then Sadheep's cousins' garage, we rented a small warehouse in Langley. Only then did I leave my employment at the restaurant. After all these years, finally I could use my training. I was euphoric. Some days I worked all through the night, filling orders, building computers — making money. When my wife and I could no longer keep up with the orders we hired employees. First it was my friend, Vishal. Then his brother. Soon we had more than twenty employees.

"Five years later, we bought a house on a quiet street off West Marine Drive. I had kept my promise. Sadheep had her fine home. We hired a housekeeper. I interviewed many applicants. I was looking for just the right one. I found her in the person of Miss Helen Campbell. She was in her forties, and although she had never married, she was very fond of children.

She came from a good family, a good Canadian family with ancestry in Scotland.

"Our company continued to prosper. Our sales doubled every 8 months. On a Monday morning in the summer of 1994 my accountant called to say that we should meet for lunch. When I arrived, he introduced me to a Mr. Fitch from an investment firm. The decision was made to go public — to sell shares in Manhas Networks. Selling shares would give us more money to grow even faster. But more than that, I would be recognized by the business community. It was an exciting time. Accountants, lawyers, investment bankers and journalists all arranging their schedules to accommodate Badra, the bus-boy. I remember the day that our company began trading on the exchange. I bought a Jaquar and drove to The Chan Dynasty for lunch.

"Of course, with the public company came more work. I was no longer just designing and selling computers for businesses. Now my day started at 6:30 when the stock exchange opened. If my company had been mentioned by someone of influence then the price would be changing. I quickly learned that my most important job was to make sure that the business journalists and analysts said nice things about us. Since I was busy making computers during the day, much of these new duties came in the evening. There was always one more meeting or dinner to go to. One more important person to meet and entertain. I had a hide-a-bed in my new office and many nights I slept there.

"My wife had been telling me for so long that she was unhappy. To me, this was not possible. We had a beautiful house, a housekeeper and private school for the girls. How could they not be happy? Some days she would say: 'I would have more companions if I were a widow.' I shrugged it off. It was to be expected. I was an executive and she didn't understand all of the demands on my time. I would fix it by buying everyone gifts. Jewellery, clothes, things — I don't remember what I bought. I had someone from the office purchase them and the courier would deliver. In June of `96 I came home after being away for two weeks. Sadheep and the children were gone. It was a total surprise. There was a notice from her attorney in the mail. What could I do? I went back to the office — to my new family — and called Mr. Fitch. 'Don't let anyone from the press hear about it for awhile.' he told me. 'It will knock the legs out from under our stock.'

"Mr. Fitch was right. When the story got out the shares plummeted. Sadheep was a major shareholder and uncertainty is death to a stock. Over the course of the next year as accountants and lawyers did their work the shares continued to drift downward. My attention was drawn away from the company and it suffered. I slowly understood the depth of my loss. I had reasoned that our company was an extension of my caring for Sadheep and the girls. With them gone, I had no interest in the company. Customers feeling my indifference began searching out new suppliers. For the first time in its brief history Manhas Networks failed to grow. When the financial reports declared a loss for the quarter, investors ran for the exit. The banks displayed their nervousness by cutting our credit. The company was failing, my dreams were shattered, and I blamed Sadheep. The divorce was bitter. When it was over, everything was gone. Manhas Networks, our fine house but most of all my Sadheep and my precious little ones. It would be years before I could rebuild what I destroyed.

"Last year, after all this time, I finally got to see them." He pulls his girls close.

"They are so beautiful — just like their mother. It was

awkward at first, but then we started to talk. I have missed out on so much. I never saw them grow-up. Not just because of our separation. Even before, with my business, I was so consumed by it. There was time for nothing else.... no one else. I remember so little of the early years." He turns and looks deeply into the eyes of his daughters. "But there are some memories, surely... some good memories." It is a statement of uncertainty. Badra is leading with his heart. "Ranjna, Rabetta tell me please. Tell me of some good memories with your foolish papa."

An awkward silence and then some careful coaxing: "Remember..... remember when we went back to India, to Jaipur and stayed at The Rambagh Palace. And Grandma came with your uncles and cousins and said how grand a hotel it was and how lucky you were. Or when we went to Disneyland and Hollywood and stayed at the Bel Aire. We saw some real movie stars. Remember?"

"Yes there were some good times pop." Ranjna takes the lead. Her eyes have rolled back ever so slightly as she searches through the recesses of her mind erasing the years and becomes once again a little girl... daddy's little girl. "Remember.... the time..." she starts slowly and then the excited child takes over. "Remember you took me to see where you worked? It was just you and me. Mom was at home with Rabetta. She was just a baby. You took me down to the restaurant, before they opened for lunch. Luigi was in the kitchen. The fat Italian cook with the big smile — we always thought it was so funny, an Italian making egg rolls. You lifted me up and I sat on the edge of the counter. He gave me two egg rolls — 'One for Bambino, one for Papa.' he said. We went across the street to Beacon Park, just the two of us and we sat and shared. We could stay until the egg rolls were gone. I took such little bites. I thought I could make the day last forever...." The words fade softly into the distance.

"And I said," continues Badra, "I wonder how many egg rolls Luigi could hide under his apron?"

"We giggled and talked." Ranjna remembers. "It was a perfect day. The sun was so bright and warm. And there was a squirrel that came right up to us and we shared some with him too. Remember Daddy? Disneyland was nice but ... that day was special. I should have eaten slower."

"And *I* remember" Rabetta joins in. "one time when Ranjna was at school and mommy was working. You came home early and picked me up from cousin Sooki's. We didn't take the bus home. You said it was a nice day and we should walk. I think you didn't have the money. We walked and walked. Remember Daddy? I got tired and you picked me up and put me on your shoulders. It was the best ride in the world. And then we found some swings in a little park. I asked for a big push and you pushed me higher and higher. I could see for a million miles. I'll always remember that day. I love you Daddy."

There are times when you know you're intruding. Charlie and Louise quietly rise and walk away unnoticed by the story-tellers. There is nothing more to ask.... nothing more need be said. They pause at the parlour doorway and look at the three. They see a father with little material possessions and his two young teachers. They see them not in the parlour but standing in front of a small trailer in a poor area. But they don't see poverty. They see a man that is in the process of regaining great riches. Louise retrieves a tissue from a pocket, wipes her eyes and hands it to Charlie.

~

The front door bursts open and Elizabeth, Louise and Charlie are confronted by a little dark skinned boy. He strides quickly to the matron of the manor with his arm outstretched. He shakes her hand vigorously and says: "Hola! Como esta?" Without waiting for a response he repeats the process with Louise and Charlie.

"Tyler! Come back here!" commands a disembodied voice from the other side of the door. Its owner appears in the person of Tammy Clarke showing signs of a long flight with two youngsters and too much luggage.

"I'm terribly sorry. He's not usually so forward. He's so excited about the snow and everything. Oh, Hola. I mean Hello! I'm Tammy. Tammy Clarke. And this is Jessica and my husband Rick.... RICK ... I guess Rick's gone to get the rest of the luggage. We have so much luggage and they insisted on opening every piece at the airport. The immigration people I mean. And you've met Tyler. Thank you so much for taking us in. I don't mean taking us in exactly...... I mean we intend to pay and all... I just mean thank you for renting us a room .... you do have extra rooms? .. not extra... I mean a room for us. We only need one ...... RICKY! Excuse me Ma'am. If you're the lady of the house, may I use your washroom?"

"I'm Elizabeth Daliwahl. Let me show you to your room upstairs. There's an en suite that you can use. Bibi will help your husband with the luggage. Tyler, Jessica, would you also like to see the room?"

"Ah. The days of travelling with the kids. Hey Lou?"

The Clarkes were settled into the large bedroom at the end of the hall on the second floor. Michael had the hide-a-bed in the study and the Fishers would occupy the master bedroom off the living room. Their hosts had moved their personal belongings to the basement where there was a furnished suite, once used by Bibi's aunt. All in all a very comfortable arrangement put together on short notice.

Charlie and Louise have returned to their room, away from the commotion of the arrival of the guests from the airport. A quiet time to reflect on the life of Badra and his children.

"What lesson can we learn from Badra's story Charlie?"

"We could have saved a lot of money by buying the kids a few egg rolls."

"Any chance of having a meaningful conversation with you, Charles Henderson? Didn't you get anything out of what he said?"

"Yes Lou. I got it. You know I was just teasing. It's amazing what kids remember as being important. Here Badra was telling himself that he was building this empire – making all this money – for his family, and they were happiest with the old Badra that had time to spend with them. If not for the family, then he would have to admit that he was working day and night for his own interests and ego and that's more difficult to acknowledge. It's a shame that he had to lose so much before he discovered the truth."

"Lose what? The house? His business?"

"No Lou. Okay I'll say it. His family was his greatest asset. And my retirement savings, or lack of them, are not the most important things in my life. There. Are you happy?"

"Oh Charlie, Daddy would be so proud of you."

6

TIME OR MONEY

"Time is the most valuable
thing a man can spend."
...Theophraties 300 B.C.

There was a knock on the bedroom door. Elizabeth
was there with an invitation. "You folks must be starving.
It's after eight. Bibi and I ate earlier with Badra and the
girls. There's nothing open in town but if you want to come
down to the kitchen we can fix something for you. I'll check
with the other guests and see if they want to join us."

In half an hour the travellers were all gathered in the
dining room. The table had seating for twelve. Bibi was
seated at the head with Elizabeth at the far end, when she
wasn't running to care for her guests. Michael was to his
right followed by Charlie and Tom. Louise was to Bibi's
left and then the four Clarkes. Florence sat next to her
husband Tom. The table was loaded with sandwiches and
sweets. The Clarkes had donated coffee which they had

brought back from the Dominican Republic.

"It's always so interesting staying at bed and breakfast places." said Florence Fisher. "You meet people from everywhere and every walk of life. Now George and I are from Saskatoon — well actually we farm near the town of Delisle. It's about 20 miles from Saskatoon but not too many people have ever heard of Delisle so we just say we come from Saskatoon. We've been there ever since we got married over forty years ago. For Tom it's been even longer 'cause he was born there, same as his father before him. Just imagine! There have been three generations of Fishers on that same piece of land outside of Delisle. It don't look like there will be a fourth. We only have the one child and she's off working in Winnipeg. She's a nurse. Smart as a whip. Practically runs the whole third floor. Never got married — not so far — but there's plenty of time. She just turned thirty and women are getting married later now. Career comes first. Not like in our days. Don't suppose she'd ever come back to the farm even when she does find a man. Not many want to farm now. There's no future in it. That's what Tom always says. Don't you Tom?"

"Have another sandwich Flo."

"That's Tom's way of telling me to stop talking. So who's next?

Before anyone could speak there was a knock at the door. Bibi went to investigate and returned a moment later with two more seeking refuge from the weather. They may have stepped out of a fashion magazine. The gentleman was Randolph Webber. His surname, to no one's surprise, was followed by *the third*. Despite having walked a hundred yards in two feet of snow when his vehicle got stuck he looked impeccable, albeit a little gaudy with the gold necklace and bracelet, at least for Charlie's taste.

"At least there are no earrings." Charlie thought.

The earrings were noticeably present on his partner. She was introduced as Gwen. They must have been on their way to a gala event where she would have been a hit. She had not fared as well walking in the snow. The boots didn't quite make it high enough to meet her leather mini. Charlie could only imagine someone walking with such restrictions. Hardly walking, he was envisioning more of a wiggle when Louise's foot found his shin under the table.

"My Hummer spun out and got hung up in a snow drift. My cell died when I was trying to call roadside assistance. Then the client pages me and says the dinner meeting is off. What a day! Can I use your phone to have someone come and get me out of here."

Several minutes later, Mr. Webber returns with the inevitable. No one will rescue him and his lady this evening. Charlie restrains a smile as he talks in his head with Charles. "They will be forced to spend the night. A pair of Rolexes among a box of Timexes."

"There is a room on the second floor, next to the Hendersons. It is one room that you will be needing?" Mrs. Daliwahl questions delicately.

"One room will be fine."

"It is *Mr. and Mrs.* Webber then?"

"Sure. Whatever. Do you take Diners Club? I have the platinum card."

"We will see to that later. My wife will show you the room and then you must come back and sit down with us." Bibi offers. The others just starting to eat some sandwiches. You say you missed your dinner. There is plenty here for two more."

Randolph and Gwen followed Elizabeth to their room and returned a few moments later to the table. Randolph presumed upon the seat vacated by Elizabeth. Gwen baulked at sitting in the empty chair by her companion. Tom offered her his chair and moved over beside Mr. Webber. Gwen praised Tom's gallantry as she accepted his offer and slid comfortably between Tom and Charlie. They obviously weren't oil executives but they were men and with a man on each side Gwen always felt comfortable. The tuna salad sandwiches were another matter. Randolph had promised her Lobster Thermidor if she came to another dreary meeting and flattered some old geezer. Tuna was a long way from lobster in Gwen's world.

Bibi went outside to bring in more wood for the fire. Elizabeth was in the kitchen brewing coffee and Florence was about to resume her quest for information about her fellow guests.

"Randolph is such a nice name. It must be English. I think we might have named our boy Randolph — if we had a boy— but we only have one child and she's a girl. Carolyne's a nurse you know. Works in Winnipeg. We wanted a boy to take over the farm but we only had the one child. What do you think Tom? If we had a son would we have named him Randolph? Fat chance! Your dad was Tom as was your great uncle and his father before him. We would have named him Tommy. Not Thomas Fisher the fourth — just Tommy. I never heard tell of a Randolph Fisher. But it would have been nice to have a Tommy at home to look after the land. But he wouldn't stay. There's no future in it. That's what Tom always says. Don't you Tom?" She didn't wait for her husband to answer. He would only tell her to have something to eat.

"So, Mr. Randolph Webber, what kind of work do you do? Charlie Henderson here works at a pulp mill and Michael Tibbetts is retired. He's from England you know. Of course you'd guess right off when you hear him.

"Little chance of hearing him or anybody else." Tom quipped. But it was no use.

"You're no farmer." Florence carried on. "I never saw a farmer dressed like that. What kind of job do you have?"

"I'm a consultant. An advisor. I help my clients to retire... like Mr. Tibbetts here."

"Oh I didn't need any help," Michael corrected. "You reach 65 and your employer says you're through. You don't need help to get old."

"Perhaps not quite like Mr. Tibbetts. My clients retire wealthy. That's where I come in." Randolph clarified. "I work with executives and professional people who require substantial amounts of money to maintain a certain life style after they stop working."

Charles heard Randolph's answer and knew his hunch was right. He was standing at the top of the stairs. He had paused on his way to get something from his room. When he first laid eyes on him there was something about Randolph Webber that was familiar. It was Charlie really, with his comment about 'Rolexes". And when Randolph had said 'consultant' and 'retirement', Charlie heard financial planner. Charles heard 'investment salesman'. By the time Randolph had given his first case history of a wealthy client living in financial bliss, Charles had returned with a notebook. In his notes was the data gathered from his session at the library. In his memory was the night spent with Carnegie, Rockefeller and Mark Twain. It was

Charles' turn to be the investigative journalist. But first he would let Randolph Webber III have his say.

"It's like this. There are only two ways to make money in this world. One way is to work for it. We all do that, but for most people, that's the only way they ever make money. But the very rich, they make most of their millions by having money work for them. So when my clients decide to stop working and retire, we keep their money working."

"Tom! That's what we need," Florence Fisher had been hanging on every word. "We need to have someone like Mr. Webber put our money to work so we can start thinking about retirement."

"Flo. First we gotta have some money. Here, have another sandwich."

"Hold on Mrs. Fisher. That's not really the way I work. You see I'm like your doctor. I can only see so many patients and ..... no. I'm more like a specialist that works only through referrals. When someone is referred to me, we set up a meeting and I determine if I can work with this particular person. I look at their present situation, what their objectives are and .....well, frankly, if we have that special chemistry that tells me that we can work together to achieve the client's objectives. It takes time..... and I have to be honest with you. I only select a few from the hundreds that I interview."

There was a sigh of disappointment from Florence Fisher. She was in the presence of a great man — a financial wizard who could lift them from a common existence to millionaire status. It was within her grasp and yet she was to be denied. 'Only a few chosen.' Surely, there was no hope of her and Tom being invited into such a select group.

Farmers from Delisle Saskatchewan, what chance did they have? And Tom hadn't helped her cause by letting Mr. Webber know they had no money.

It wasn't even true. They had *some* money. No. Not in their farm account. The last few years had made sure of that. What with the price of grain being what it is; and then the poor crops. Every farmer in the district was hurting. Except the Andersons — and they weren't really farmers. They spent more time with bankers, lawyers and accountants than on the land.

"But you do seem like the type of people that I could help." Randolph was leaning towards Florence as he spoke, offering a flicker of hope. "And that's what my business is really all about — helping people. People like Charlotte Wicker. A number of years ago she came into my office and asked for some advice. She was a single mom living in a one bedroom apartment with three little kids." Randolph holds up three fingers to emphasize the point. Gwen makes a face at the thought of children which draws looks of amusement from Rick and Tammy Clarke.

"She'd saved up $500 to put towards buying a place of their own. But what can you do with five hundred bucks? Hey Gwen, isn't that about what your skirt cost? Imagine what it would have set me back if it came down to your knees!" Randolph leads off with a laugh but stops when the others fail to join in. Gwen enjoys the attention and responds to the looks by crossing her legs. Charlie knows better than to stare.

"So Charlotte Wicker puts $500 on my desk and asks if I can make it grow. I told her just what I told you, Florence. I wasn't taking any new clients. She then took out a picture of her kids and laid it down beside the money and said; 'Please Mr. Webber. If not for me, then for the children. Do it for the children.'

"What could I do? I invested the money in a deal that I had put together for some of my bigger clients. Oh sure, Charlotte's money didn't buy many units and she really didn't qualify to be in on the deal; but I didn't see the obstacles, just the children, and my chance to help. When it paid off, I took the profits and rolled it into another deal. And another.

"Charlotte called me just last week to say she bought a four bedroom house in Eagle Ridge Estates. That'll make three houses she owns and her oldest boy Harry is in his second year med."

Charlie was sure he could see the tears welling up in Randolph's eyes. Behind the Ralph Loren designer frames.

"I can't promise you Florence, but if you and Tom call my office I'll have my assistant schedule you for an interview." He pulled a business card from a gold embossed case and pressed it in Florence's hand. She glowed like it was prom night, clutched the card and said softly:

"Do it for my Tommy, Mr. Webber. Do it for Tommy."

~

Tom was about to offer his wife another sandwich when Bibi entered from the parlour. He had been tending the fire. Charlie was sure that he had heard him speaking with a man. He was just as sure that Badra had retired to his room some time earlier.

"Elizabeth, we will need to make up another bed for Jim here. One more stranded traveller for the night." Jim Larsen made his appearance. Charlie wouldn't have been surprised if he had ridden a quarter horse into the manor. He was probably close to 70 but it was hard to guess his age, for it was a face that had spent a good deal of time outdoors and its owner didn't look the type to put much faith in regular maintenance. In his hand was a leather Stetson that had been mauled over the years. His heavy coat was one of those all purpose shelters that Charlie only ever saw on Westerns. It was a matched set with the hat.

Bibi went through the customary introductions. There had been no knock at the door. Jim had seen Bibi in the shed gathering wood and made inquiries about staying. The inn was officially full, but you don't turn away strangers on a night like this. They were in the hospitality business. Like many immigrants who had struggled to learn the English language, Bibi had learned not just the meaning of the words but the origin. "Hospitality," he had explained to Elizabeth when they opened Bow River Manor. "Hospitality means the love of strangers." They would find a spare bed.

Michael quickly made a suggestion. "There's plenty of room in the den with me — if you can scare up another cot. If it's all right with you Jim?"

"Have you had all your shots? Jim raises one eye brow as he gives Michael the once over — playing for the audience. Then he continues, "Wasn't planning on no sleep over. I was doing fine. Woulda been alright if there hadn't been that big ugly tank in the middle of the road. The city musta called out the army. Never saw such a thing. I'll have to straighten out the bumper on my truck when I get home. Someone's gonna need to slap some paint on the tank."

Mr. Randolph Webber III blanched. The tears were still there but they were no longer for his client.

"Gotcha!" Jim slapped Randolph smartly across the shoulder blades. "Bibi here told me about your fancy four wheeler stuck in the snow. I was havin some fun with ya. I'da made it home but ran outta gas. But I came prepared." He reached inside the folds of his coat and produced a 40 ouncer of Captain Morgan's. He glanced over at his host and offered a deal. "I'll trade you some of this for a sandwich or two."

Bibi had reclaimed his position at the head of the table. Rick Clarke had taken Jessica and Tyler off to bed. Louise had moved down to sit directly across from Charlie where her foot would reach with ease. Florence, seeking to escape the continual offers of food from Tom moved across to Randolph's right. She had another reason for the move. She suggested that Tom move down closer to Mr. Webber and give Mrs. Webber a little more room. Charlie thought he heard the emphasis on the *Mrs.*. Of course when Tom moved, Gwen replaced him with an invitation to the latest arrival. Jim shook out his coat and threw it and his hat in a corner and took the chair beside Gwen. When Elizabeth returned she took Louise's former place to the left of her husband. Rick soon returned and resumed his place next to Tammy. The seating was complete. Twelve strangers drawn together by a late winter storm and the kindness of the Daliwahls.

With Jim's arrival the conversation had changed from Randolph Webber's infomercial on the humanitarian values of capitalism to the mundane topics of politics, taxes and the weather. Especially the weather. Randolph had been shaken by Jim's tale of side-swiping his Hummer and ventured out to check on the vehicle. Rick and Tammy talked with enthusiasm of their volunteer work in the third

world and the educating of Tyler and Jessica. Louise told
stories about her folks.. By the time Randolph returned
from his vehicle inspection the topic returned to money.
But it wasn't Randolph who did the talking. It was Michael.

~

Michael lives in Victoria on Vancouver Island.
More precisely he lives in Esquimalt, a sister city to
Victoria, across the Johnson Street Bridge. When you think
of Esquimalt, you think of the naval base. With the cut-
backs in military spending, the city has lost some of it's
shine. That can be a good thing if you're looking to find a
cost efficient place to live. He's a former shopkeeper from
England. He came to Canada 20 years ago after his
marriage failed. "My missus was lonely. The shop was
open seven days a week. I didn't want to hire anyone. I
wanted the money for our golden years."

After immigrating, Michael worked as a clerk until
retirement. It seems hard to imagine him retired. He looks
young and full of energy. Charlie remembers how he
entered the manor. His four weeks of luggage for Mexico
was in a back pack that he carried effortlessly.

"When I reached 65, they turned me out to pasture.
But I don't mind. I've been at work since I was 13. I had a
bit of money put aside. It was enough to convince the bank
to go halves with me in buying a little place.

"I get by on the Old Age Security and my Canada
Pension. There's a little comes in from England — just
enough to make sure that I get no supplement, but like I
said: I get by. Others in the complex are bringing in more
money. I'll ring one of `em up and ask if he fancies going
for a pint and he'll say: 'I can't afford it.' Can't afford it...

and he's making more than me! And I know why. If you visit me you won't see a car in my drive. That's the ticket. Everyone of 'em has a car... but not me. Pete's always on about; 'why don't you get yourself a car'. I'd sooner be able to eat lunch at Schooners Pub or run off to Mexico whenever I fancy. That's why."

Michael buys a senior's bus pass for $65 for the year. He rarely uses it. He says he walks. With his energy, Charlie sees him jogging.

"He's right you know." Elizabeth joins in. "There's all this talk about the high cost of living. But we haven't seen it, have we Bibi?"

"It depends on how you spend your money. Like the chairs we're sitting on. These old chairs need a little attention now and then. Every forty years the glue gives up. But at least you can fix them." We've had these since the kids were small. Mind you, I don't really know how old they are. We didn't buy them new, did we Bess?"

"No, we've hardly bought anything new. A few years ago, used furniture could be picked up for next to nothing. Now they call it antiques and triple the price. I guess we've done all right with these old pieces, but at the time it was all we could afford."

"Without going into debt," Bibi adds. "Elizabeth is dead-set against going into debt. We were the last ones in our group of friends to get a television. We waited until we had the money."

"Then we bought a used one. It was only a year old but it had been repossessed. We got it for half price and it lasted us for years. Whoever paid the other half only got to use it for a year. We tell our kids the reason that we could retire early was that we never went into debt for things we didn't need. Bibi never made big money but we managed just fine. The trouble with younger people is they forget how long their parents worked and saved for all the things that they see around them. Then when they get a place of their own, they feel they should have everything that mom and dad have."

"The advertisers make sure of that." Bibi continues, "And the banks and finance companies are right there to help them into debt."

"The joy of owing no money is the extra control you have over your life. A few years ago when things got slow at work, I opted for early retirement. I got a buy-out and the younger fellows got to keep their jobs. I didn't get a king's ransom but we used it to open the manor. We're open for the summer. If we ever get tired of it, we'll sell and get something smaller, but for now it's a great way to meet people. With the income from this, a little interest from our savings, and my early Canada Pension we're bringing in $1500 per month. That's enough for our lifestyle."

"I don't know what we'll do with the extra when we turn 65 and we qualify for the OAS."

"Well on $1500 a month you can't do anything. You must stay at home every night with the lights out." Randolph had never heard of such nonsense and challenged the mere possibility of subsisting on such a meagre income.

"Oh no. We are active in the community... and we travel."

"How far can you travel on $1500 a month? You can't get out of the city on your budget."

"Well, we just got back from a month in England. You see we have friends and the odd cousin over there.

They visit us here and we pay them a visit every now and then. We just watch for a cheap flight. Our friends acted as our tour guides. And we're not into lavish meals in restaurants. Travel is really about seeing the country and meeting the locals. It doesn't cost much if you're careful."

"Time out!" Randolph gestures with a hand signal to end Elizabeth's experience. "Okay, I get it. Michael, your attempt at being an entrepreneur failed in England. You came over here, played it safe, and put in your time until you qualified for the government pension, and now you have enough to exist, if you deny yourself a normal lifestyle.

"And you, Bibi and Elizabeth, you gave up before you got forced out of your job, and manage to lead a quiet, and I might add, boring life that you can afford if you patch-up someone elses discarded items and call visiting relatives an exotic vacation.

"But let's get real. Doesn't everyone want to be rich? Oh I know most of us won't come right out and say it, but if we're really honest with ourselves; doesn't each and every one of us desire to be wealthy." He knows the Fishers are silently agreeing. Their heads are nodding ever so slightly.

"Michael, don't you wish that your corner store had grown into a Wal-Mart? And Bibi don't you get sick of glueing together your furniture and looking for sales? Admit it. We all want to be rich. Why else are we so intensely interested in the lives of the very rich? Because we imagine that we, somehow— one day, could be living that life. We dream and scheme to see our fantasies fulfilled; we take chances even when the odds of winning are ridiculous.

"And here we are, living in a country where everyone has an opportunity to work and invest and make their dreams of being rich come true. It's fine to accept a minimum existence if things don't work out, but don't expect me to see you as a role model. People come to me to help them create wealth and that's a valuable service for them — and for the country."

Michael and Bibi were answering simultaneously.

"Oh I've regrets all right. But not about the store. I regret that I lost my missus over the store."

"And I enjoy fixing things. I suppose the same as some people enjoy making money or building a business. But you're wrong, Mr. Webber, about Bess and I not being rich. To be rich means having an abundance. You should see our family and all our friends when we're together for special occasions. You will not find anyone richer among all of your clients."

"Could I add something?" Rick Clarke had been nodding in agreement with Michael and the Daliwahls. "Tammy and I have worked on volunteer projects in a few countries over the past four years. We pay our way over and back but while we're in the country we are housed and fed. We just finished working on a new community hospital with workers from several countries and scores of locals. So we get to travel and work together and help others. That's a big change for us.

"Before Jessica was born, we were your typical DINKS." The word draws puzzled looks from everyone over 50. Florence has her hand over her mouth; a gesture that Tom wishes she would practice more often.

"You know — dual income no kids." Rick explains. We were living in Edmonton. I was an ambulance attendant and Tammy was a medical receptionist. At the time, we pretty much agreed with what Randolph just said. Even before I left school the talk was about getting a good job, which meant high-paying, and retiring as millionaires by age forty. We were earning over $60,000 but there was never extra money. I just thought the savings would start after we had all the things that my parents had. Until then we just lived pay day to pay day. As our income had increased we increased our spending — a bigger house, a second car, more toys just like Bibi said. When Tammy got pregnant I thought she'd take a couple months off with maternity leave, then the baby would go to day care and we'd carry on. That's the way all our friends did it. That's the way it was at our house when I was growing up.

  "My dad's been at Schneiders for over thirty years. He'll retire with a good pension in two years. Mom still works for the city. Geoff, my step dad, drives a truck. When we were growing up my sister and I would go over to the neighbour's after school. Lots of kids were doing the same. We just figured that's how it worked. Mom and Dad would get home before six and we'd eat a little later unless they picked up something on the way home. Weekends were family time ....until the divorce. Then it was evenings with Mom and every other weekend with Dad. Geoff came along after a couple of years. I was in high school. Lots of my friends were going through the same thing. Some kids were with their mom and others were with their dad. Then there were the parents' boyfriends and girlfriends coming and going. It made for some interesting parent-teacher interviews. We used to joke around in the locker room that the government should do away with Father's Day because of the confusion. I tried living with my dad for a year but it didn't work out and my mom wasn't happy about the idea.

"By the time Jessica arrived, we had decided to be different. Tammy and I didn't want to be like my family when I was growing up. When I was young and going over to the neighbour's, I often wondered why my mom couldn't be the lady who stayed at home and looked after the kids. We thought that maybe if we watched our spending, Tammy could stay at home — at least part time. Or maybe she could replace some of her income by caring for other children at home. We really didn't know how it would work, but we wanted to try. By the time Tammy's maternity leave was over she had told her employer she wasn't coming back.

"Our income was now $37,000. After a year we were surprised that we were still living much like before. Yes we made some changes but not as drastic as I feared. We were eating at home more but with the new baby we would be doing that even with more money. We had sold Tammy's car, and yes Michael, this did free up a lot of extra income. I no longer had my membership at the gym but Jessica kept me active. And as for the 200 cable stations, I can't believe I ever had the time to watch all that television.

"What little sacrifices we made paled in comparison to the joy and satisfaction we derived from being Jessica's parents. When Tammy discovered that she was pregnant with Tyler I began looking for ways to spend more time at home. I couldn't see how we could cut back any more. In fact, I thought with another mouth to feed I might have to start taking on a little overtime. And then a week before Tyler was born I met Chris Munroe.

"I was working days with my partner Ted when we got a call to transport Chris to Woodgrove. We picked him

up at Royal Alexander, finished all the paper work and
started the drive. Woodgrove was outside our district and
I'd never been there. The directions showed it to be about
80 miles. With the traffic it would take at least two hours.
The first part of the trip was pretty routine. Ted and I were
talking with an ear on the radio to monitor where the other
units were. Our patient had been sedated for the trip. After
an hour Chris started coming around. He was a little
disoriented so I went back to settle him down. I introduced
myself and reminded him where he was going. That seemed
to calm him and I was all set to slide back in the cab with
Ted when Chris started to talk:

"'Rick, do you ever work any overtime at this job?'

"'Sure. Everyone does a little. We're having another
child soon and I might do a bit more. Why do you ask?'

"'Well don't do it! I worked overtime most of my life
and it's not worth it. I was a guard at Edmonton Maximum
for 28 years. Not too many guys hang in for that long.'

"'You must have enjoyed it.' I concluded.

"'Nope.' Chris contradicted. 'Hated it with a
passion. But the pay and benefits were good. And I knew
that with enough overtime banked I could get out early with
all the money that the financial experts say you need for a
rich retirement. I volunteered for every extra shift. If it was
a holiday so much the better. I was pulling down triple time
some shifts. My wife used to complain that I was the one in
prison, doing time. She had a get out of jail free card from
the Monopoly board game enlarged and framed and gave it
to me on our anniversary. I took it to work and hung it in my
office.

"'On my breaks I read all the financial advice books.
I subscribed to saving 10% of my wages and when it didn't

grow fast enough I started saving 20%. My wife thinks I haven't had a raise in ten years. I've just been stashing the extra away for our retirement.'

"'So Chris you must be almost there?'

"'Oh I'm there all right.' I can still hear Chris say that. Then he told me the rest. 'A year ago I had this lump on my leg. My wife was after me to get it looked at but it's so hard to get in to see a GP and I didn't want to take off any time. Besides after awhile it almost went away — at least it wasn't getting any bigger, and I don't go running to a doctor with every little thing. I figured I'd have plenty of time to sit around in waiting rooms later in the year when I retired at 55.

"'Rick, I'm there all right. We've got a beautiful house in Willow Park, free and clear. We've got a cottage on Gabriola Island on the west coast. I've got a 34 foot motor home sitting in the drive that's hardly been used. I've got a couple a hundred thousand in Canada Savings Bonds. And just like the experts promised, I'll have a million bucks in my RRSP before I'm 65. And this month I'm officially retired with full pension.

"'And...' I knew there was another "and"

"'And I got at best one month left to enjoy it. Oh I'm there all right.' Chris closed his eyes and rolled away from me and everything else. I found out that Woodgrove was a palliative care facility. I drove out to see Chris the next week on my day off, but I was too late.

"I never worked another hour of overtime. After Tyler was born, we sold our house in Edmonton, paid off our mortgage and bought a little place in Hanna with the balance. I drive courier a couple days a week. That's when we're not volunteering. Our expenses are really low and we even get some help. Being a low income family, the government sends us about five hundred dollars every month in child benefits. Our family has the one ingredient that my sister and I never had with our parents when we were growing up — time. You hear busy parents say ' I'm taking an hour and spending some quality time with my child.' as if parenting is an activity like playing golf. Once a week you take a lesson from a pro and then practice for an hour. When you're done the clubs go back in your garage until next week. You can't schedule a child's life into a time slot that fits your career and social life. I'm not knocking parents who, due to circumstances, need to work the hours they do; but I think many of us fall into a lifestyle because we haven't considered any alternatives."

7

TAXING DIFFERENCES

"The income tax laws have
made more liars of Americans
than golf.".....Will Rogers

Randolph has been impatiently waiting for Rick to
finish so that he could once again confront the story tellers.
He was not accustomed to spending an evening with those
who espoused the beauty of simple living. As a vice
president of Creative Capital, an aggressive brokerage
firm, he lived in the rough and tumble world of risk and
reward and winner take all. With each new raconteur he had
refilled his glass from Jim's bottle. Charlie had watched his
colour redden as the blood vessels enlarged and made their
appearance closer to the surface. Was it the liquor or the
stories? With the conclusion of Rick Clarke's experience,
Randolph's displeasure was vented.

"That's where all my tax dollars are going!" He
exploded. "I'm working my butt off so that Ottawa can send

you money to stay home and play with your kids." He turns his attention to the Daliwahls "Or so you can take early retirement, and arrange to qualify as a needy senior, grasping for handouts while you drain my Canada Pension Plan. What happened to everyone paying their fair share? We've got too many people feeding at the tax trough. The few of us who are working end up supporting everyone else. That's what's wrong with our tax system!"

The room was silent. Everyone was rethinking their position. Charlie waded in assuming a moderator's role. He tried to imagine what Mark Twain might say.

"And you thought I had issues, Louise. He does raise some good points. And I've thought of a couple of my own. Anyone care to respond? Elizabeth? Rick?"

"Randolph, do you use an accountant?" inquired Elizabeth.

"Macpherson with Macpherson and Kilpatrick, the best CA firm in the city."

"And probably the most expensive."

"You get what you pay for. I'm a professional and I only work with professionals at my level..... with my standards." Randolph was always selling, even when answering a simple question.

"And what do you get?" Elizabeth pursued.

"What?"

"What do you get? You said 'you get what you pay for.' I'm interested in just what are you paying for. When you hire Mr. Macpherson as your accountant, what does he do for you to warrant you paying him his fee?"

"What every accountant does. He does my books and files tax returns."

"And how do you come to have such a high opinion

of his firm. That they are the best in the city? How do you measure such a thing?"

"By reputation. You hear things. The type of work they do. The favourable decisions they win with Canada Customs and Revenue. The amount of taxes you save. But surely you must know all this?"

"Yes Mr. Webber, I know this. I was just verifying that you did. I wanted to be sure that you realized that you hire someone to help you pay as little income tax as possible. You see, I thought for a moment that you were lecturing us for not paying enough taxes. But I must have misunderstood. Because you actually pay someone to help you do the same thing."

A response was on his tongue. His mouth was partially open when he paused and turned his attention to his glass. He refilled it and played with the remnants of ice, watching them melt as he searched for his answer staring into the glass cupped in his hands. Jim reached over and withdrew the bottle to insure there would be some for later. Randolph had bought some time and was ready.

"Not the same thing. I pay tens of thousands of dollars every year. Much more than my share. It's only right that I should pay less. Ricky here, not only pays no tax, he gets money every month from my taxes so he can go spend it in some other country. I thought communism was dead?"

"I play by the rules. We didn't lobby Ottawa to give us the family allowance. We don't even pay someone to find ways to pay less or get more. Sure, I pay very little income tax. We were paying thousands every year when Tammy and I had full time jobs. We chose to earn less. You could too Randolph. But you have to decide to spend less and change your priorities as to what's important, and what makes you happy."

"If those are the rules, then the rules have to change.

Just imagine what would happen if everyone decided to
slough off and work two days a week, pay no taxes and look
for handouts." Randolph wasn't finished. "This country
wasn't build by people sitting on their duff."

"I was not born here," says Bibi, "but I was of the
impression that this wonderful country was build by
families working together. There are many kinds of work
that people do that is not in exchange for money. To
determine a man's worth by his income level or the amount
of income taxes he pays is to deny the contributions of
many great painters and composers. And what of those who
changed the world like Gandhi and Jesus Christ? These
men were not high income earners."

"Great stuff!" Charlie whispered to his alter ego. But
it was Louise that won the day.

"Tell me Randolph, which of these persons is the
better citizen? The lawyer earning $400,000 per year and
paying $150,000 in income tax, or a single mom who pays
no tax and collects government benefits totaling $17,000?"

"No contest. Give me the lawyer any day."

"Take your time Mr. Webber. We need to find out a
little more about our contestants."

"Our lawyer attended a Canadian university for six
years to earn a law degree. The cost to the taxpayer was
$50,000."

"Wrong! No cost. An investment that will multiply
in value. He starts paying taxes with his first paycheck."

"First he has to article with a law firm. At minimal
pay. The interest deductions for student loans means he
pays no taxes for the next couple of years." Louise spoke
with authority. Charlie's eyes were fixed on her. Was this
the woman he had been married to for thirty years?

"Okay, agreed. Our lawyer doesn't pay much tax until he's licenced. But he makes up for it. Remember? Now he's paying $150,000 per year."

"Not so fast. Our lawyer is ambitious. After a few years he follows the money into the States. Of course he pays no taxes to Canada while he's there. Our investment in Mr. Lawyer is paying dividends to a foreign country. He makes a name for himself as a criminal lawyer and after several years he returns with his wife and child."

"And pays big taxes."

"And now, he pays big taxes. But let's leave our lawyer for a moment and cross the tracks and meet our single mom with two children. She didn't always live here. Three years ago there was a small house in a nicer part of town with a picket fence and a husband who worked hard to provide for them. He was a mechanic. He dreamed of owning the foreign cars that he worked on. One day he meets the owner of a 500 SL. He's flattered when the man in the nice clothes takes an interest in him. His new friend offers to give him a chance to improve himself, meet some more of the right people. The right people happen to deal in drugs and it isn't long before our mechanic, husband and father is introduced to the drug world. First as an occasional user, then to pay for his acquired habit, his new friends show him how he can make some quick extra money. Even before the arrest and job loss, our mechanic and his family are in trouble. Their fairytale marriage is ending. The late nights, missed suppers, mood swings and abusive behaviour as the drugs alienate her husband, send our young mother first to her parents, and then to a community shelter.

"Our young family has descended from a modest

income family, paying employment insurance and medical premiums, Canada Pension.... and yes some Income Tax, to a dysfunctional unemployed drug abuser with an arrest record and a homemaker with two children supported by the government."

"What did I tell you. A pathetic drain on society. Give me the lawyer."

"Our lawyer is having some marital problems of his own. His busy career has demanded most of his time. To fill the void his wife has taken up a career of her own. The children have a nanny. The husband finds someone more compatible in his office; someone he sees much more often than his wife. His wife is not surprised or even upset. She too has found someone more attuned to her new lifestyle. The divorce is amicable. The lawyer gets the cars, boat and dogs; the wife gets the house and custody of the child. The child gets to keep the nanny."

"You can bet the lawyer fees are not paid for out of the public purse like your other couple," Randolph quips.

"Not the lawyer fees. And he even pays some of the court costs. But who pays the rest? The judges' salaries, and those of the clerks and the myriads of other administrative expenses? And who picks up the tab for the social and emotional costs to yet another child?

"There's one more detail we need to know. How does our lawyer earn his fees? Let's enter the offices of his firm. Go past the receptionist, down the hall, past the boardroom with the oriental rugs and original works of art. Enter the corner office overlooking the downtown and see our lawyer with a client. Does the client look familiar? Well tanned, impeccably dressed, his Mercedes is parked below. The same Mercedes that our young mechanic envied.

"Now let's look at the balance sheet. On one side we have a high income earner who, after having his education financed by the taxpayer in the amount of $50,000, is now contributing $150,000 towards government revenue. But what does he cost the system in order to earn his $400,000 from drug dealers to help keep them in business? What is the cost in addiction treatment, policing, crown attorneys and judges? What is the cost in communities, families and lives?

"On the other side of the balance sheet we have a mother caring for two children. She adds nothing to government coffers. The province pays $14,000 per year and she receives a further $3,000 from the federal and provincial governments for child care. Before you write her off as an expensive burden, ask yourself: 'Could society care for these children any cheaper by putting them in an institution?' The year her husband was in jail, taxpayers were billed $44,000 for his care. By comparison our single mom is a bargain. As a bonus, imagine her teaching the children to be responsible, caring members of the community. With any luck they will grow up to be successful members of society, earning lots of money and paying taxes. We can always use more lawyers."

"Are you telling me that every successful lawyer......."

"No. Of course not." Louise didn't wait for Randolph to finish. "I'm merely saying that we can't judge the value of someone's contribution to society by the amount of their cheque to Canada Customs and Revenue. The villain needn't be a lawyer — although lawyers are my favourite villains. I could have used an executive in a publicly traded corporation. And I don't just mean the ones who bilk shareholders out of their life savings and end up paying a fine or spending six months playing golf in minimum security.

"There are hundreds of corporate big wigs who greenmail their way into communities promising jobs in exchange for tax free property and huge cash incentives for every job they create. When you add in the loan guarantees and federal and provincial tax credits to these corporations you often wonder if it wouldn't be cheaper for the taxpayer to have the workforce drawing welfare. Of course it's all mostly legal and the lawyers, accountants and business journalists write glowing accounts of these nation builders. The executives may have paid millions in taxes on their personal salaries and bonuses, donated further millions to charities and political causes — at the taxpayers expense— but in the final analysis have they contributed as much as our single mother?

"And I don't mean to point fingers Mr. Webber, but doesn't your industry promote all kinds of tax funded investments for dubious ventures that have a reputation for wasting public money while financing the opulent lifestyles of the promoters."

Charles smiles with pride as he remembers why he'd married that country bumpkin from Saskatchewan.

∼

The night is wearing on. From time to time, one of the guests checks outside. Each time the report is the same. The weather forecasters had it right. The system dumping snow over most of the prairies had stalled and there was little let-up in sight. The sandwiches had been pretty well picked over. They were on a third pot of coffee.

The previous stories had divided the occupants of the manor into two camps. Those like their hosts, who lived comfortably and oblivious to the threat of inflation and government cutbacks. And those championed by Randolph Webber, who was chasing the American dream of unlimited wealth and the things and power that accompany it. Somewhere in the mix were the Fishers. Charlie had taken on the roles of moderator and official observer, but he was far from a detached observer when it came to money. He watched the protagonists and spectators as points were made. Tom and Florence Fisher had shown a decided interest in Mr. Webber's acumen for creating riches. But Charlie had caught each of them nodding in agreement as the others presented their experiences.

And then there was Gwen. She showed as much interest in the debates as she did in the sandwiches. Oh, there were some brief signs of life when the other women were glaring warnings at their husbands. She had smiled as Charlie winced each time Louise's foot had made contact with his shin. But that was hours ago. No one had paid her much attention lately, with all this talk about retirement and taxes. It wasn't that she lacked interest in money. She could listen to anyone talk about all the money they had. And if on occasion there was some indication that some of this money might be spent on her ... well naturally that would gain her attention ....and affection. But who could listen to constant babble about taxes and the heresy of living without money? When would the conversation change to clothes or jewelry? Now that was something interesting.

8

MONEY
SLAVE OR MASTER?

"Men for the sake of getting
a living forget to live."
-- Margaret Fuller

"Maybe one of you with all the answers can solve my problem." Apart from his initial teasing of Randolph, Jim has been only an observer. He had made quick work of several sandwiches, then a brownie, followed by a raspberry tart. For the past hour he followed the stories back and forth. At times he had closed his eyes, but Charlie knew it was meditation more than sleep.

"What is your problem Jim Larsen?" Bibi questioned.

"His problem is that Randy here has polished off most of his rum." Gwen was tired of being ignored.

"Oh I got more where that come from. I told you I was prepared." Jim produced another bottle from his trusty coat which had been hung on a rack in the hall.

"I want a new truck and it's $45,000, but that's most of what I get for a year."

"$45,000 is a pretty good pension," Charlie offers. He's relieved that Jim has that much money coming in. If there's a mall handy they could go shopping in the morning for a new hat. "Must be a nice truck ..." Charlie never gets to finish.

"No. Not pension money. Oh sure, I get a little of that Canada Pension and believe it or not, I'm old enough to get the Old Age cheque. That mostly goes for property taxes, gas for my truck and cat food. You wouldn't believe how much I pay the city in taxes since they started putting subdivisions in around my place.

"But no proper pension. Shucks, I never had a job with a pension. Never really had a proper job. Not one that I kept for more than a couple of months. Couldn't keep my mouth shut. Always telling the boss to do things differently. I finally just gave up and went to work for myself. Still didn't get along with the boss." He's laughing loud enough that Tammy goes to check on the children. "I'm talking about my dividends. I get $45,000 in dividends a year from TransAlta and I'm telling you that if I buy the truck, I won't have enough money left to live on."

Randolph sits upright in his chair. He's looking beyond the tattered clothes and grizzled face. There may be a friend here after all! "Mr. Larsen, you've got a million bucks in TransAlta?"

"Bingo!" shouts Jim, and Charlie sees a pair of smiles. First on Jim, then Randolph.

"Well the answer is simple enough," At least to Charles. "TransAlta shares are trading at about sixteen bucks.... right? If you sell a little less than 3000 of your shares you can buy yourself a truck."

"Can't."

"Are they yours?" There's something here Charlie — and Charles — just can't figure out.

"I said so didn't I?"

"Oh, you're saving them for your estate. Look Jim, let your kids fight over $45,000 less and spend..."

"It's the taxes. You'll be slaughtered when you sell. But I think I've got the answer." Randolph was only guessing, but Charles was sure he would work any answer into a sales presentation.

"Don't have any kids, never married. And I don't know much about taxes."

"So what are you saving it for?"

"It's hard to explain." Jim has left his chair. He's rubbing his two-day beard and pacing. He has thought of the question before, but never came up with a good enough answer. "All I know is I always wanted to have a million bucks. I scrimped and saved and did without, and now I got it, and if I buy the truck I won't have the million. I worked too hard to get it and I don't want to see it gone."

"But who gets it when *you're* gone?" Charlie questioned.

"Now that's another problem. I've got a brother, but he can't handle money. Why, when my uncle Svend died and left us each ten thousand dollars, he had it spent before I could cash my cheque. And his family's worse."

He leans over and confides in Gwen, "I've really only got my cats. Do you know anyone who would promise me to look after 13 cats if they got all my money? The city's already fussin about my cats and I ain't even gone yet." His stage whisper is heard by all and in quick succession they vote for their favourite animal shelter. Jim had already discounted them as wasteful. He wanted a good home for his cats but equally important was a good home for his money.

Charlie had to admit it. When Jim talked about his attachment to his money, Charlie could see himself. Well, he could certainly see Charles. He had grown up respecting money and that was a good thing. He'd defend that position to the death. But he could see in Jim that respect had blossomed into a possessive love, and surely that could not be healthy. Louise thought Charlie spent too much time talking about money, worrying about money. It's true they had never gone without, there had always been enough, but what about the future? It was a fact that there would be many more seniors in the future. The government may have enough funds to ensure that Louise's folks are provided for, but what about when he and Louise are in their eighties? What then? Isn't it irresponsible not to have money set aside for future use?

Charlie can feel Louise looking his way. After thirty years of marriage she knows what he's thinking, and Charlie is equally sure of what's on her mind. She's thinking about her dad. He can see her dad leaning back in his chair, smothered in kids, and he knows how the two of them would answer Jim:

"Money, like so many possessions takes effort to acquire. Then once we possess it, it takes looking after. It's a responsibility, and if we're not careful it takes on a life of its own. A little money can buy some comforts and a measure of security. But if you're not careful it can make you very insecure. You need to take extra precautions to safeguard it. Folks might think you to be a fool if you never saved any money, but what would they think if you had all this money, and then lost it? What if it's stolen? What if the bank defaults or the stock markets collapse? Where do you put it so it's not all taxed? Who gets the money when you die? Will it be fairly distributed? Do you have real friends or is it the money?"

Charles pondered over this last question as Jim said goodnight and followed Elizabeth to the den off the parlour. A few minutes later he returned and, without a word, picked up the second bottle of rum — the full one — off the table and headed back to his room. Gwen caught him before he reached the door and whispered something about a life long affection for cats.

9

FARMING, VEGAS
AND OTHER VICES

"There are three easy ways of losing money:
gambling is the quickest, women the most
pleasant, and farming the most certain."...Lord Amherst

Jim's departure is the cue for the other guests. Amid a chorus of weather predictions and speculation on road conditions, the dining room cleared, as one after another retired for the night.

"That was quite a performance you gave downstairs," Randolph had held back his scorn until they were hidden in their room.

"It wouldn't have been necessary if your performance wasn't so pitiful. 'Do it for the children.' Really. You don't seriously believe that anyone falls for that garbage? Even some penniless farmer could see through you. One of us has to go where the money is. All I did was give that rich old tramp something to dream about. And you know Randy, I could keep him a lot warmer than those mangy cats."

"Look who's calling someone a tramp," Randolph Webber pulled a spare blanket from the foot of the bed and opted to spend the night on the Lazy Boy.

~

Downstairs in the master bedroom the Fishers were mulling over the events of the evening. They were in their early sixties. Life had been good to Tom and Florence. She had married the quiet young man that came to the store for supplies. She had been the new girl in town. Her dad had lost his job in Saskatoon, and after weeks of searching, he had been hired as the manager of the Co-op in Delisle. Such a small store. Nothing like the proper department store in the city where he had worked for so many years. And the town, there wasn't even a theatre, and no high school. Florence had made plans on the day they arrived, that she was moving back to the city the first chance she got. Then she met Tom and she forgot all about the city, theatres, and even the bus ride to the high school. It really wasn't *that small* a town. They'd married when she finished school.

Tom had brought her home to the small two bedroom bungalow that he and his dad had built. He had started drawing plans for their house the day he first saw Florence at the Co-op. It was two years later that the house was finished; and another six months before he had worked up the courage to ask Florence to be his wife. He and Florence had lived there most of their married life. They brought Carolyne home when she was four days old and she had the same bedroom until she went away to nursing school. When Tom's mom took sick and couldn't climb the stairs, they had traded houses.

And so Tom and his bride started out under the watchful eye of his folks, who lived just fifty yards away in the original farmhouse, where they had begun their life together. In no time, Florence was taking her turn operating farm equipment, hauling grain to the elevator, or running errands in town. When Carolyne came along her life was complete. Her friends had chided her for being so happy, stuck in the house, tied to a toddler, and at the beck and call of her husband, but she knew better.

They were partners — equal partners. Her happiness was tied up with making Tom and Carolyne happy and she was proud of her role, her career. Often she'd stood at the window watching her husband walking in the fields; talking with his dad and the land. Her friends in Saskatoon laughed when she told them. Oh sure, they carried on conversations with their dogs and cats. One even admitted to talking to her prize roses— but talking to land?

Tom had been a farmer all his life. How many of us live the dreams of childhood? And he had wanted nothing more than to be a farmer, like his father and his father's father. Stewards — guardians of the land. To the Fishers, land was not something to subdue and squeeze every last dollar from. It was held in trust, to be nurtured and protected.

Yes, life had been good. Then two years ago his dad died. Died in the field on the 2nd of June. Tom had found him half leaning against a large boulder in the middle of the eighty acres of new barley in the north-east quarter. Leaning against the buffalo rock that had been there when herds of bison roamed the prairies and scratched away tufts of matted hair on the face of the granite. It had been there when much of the prairie had been submerged by a great lake and then receded slowly over time, leaving as a legacy the dark rich soil. Soil that grew grain in abundance and earned the area the title of 'the breadbasket of the world' when Tom's granddad had homesteaded.

He was propped up against the rock; his eyes softly closed like Tom had seen him a hundred times before. He had dozed off for the last time. In his hand was a blade of fresh grass. Tom had sat down beside his dad and picked a blade for himself. And like his father showed him, over half a century earlier, he held it between his thumbs and blew softly through the edge creating a mournful sound. And then one last time he had talked with his dad, as tears trickled through the dust on his face, spilling to the earth, further nurturing the land.

It was then, for the first time, that Tom Fisher faced the inevitable. He too would leave the land and who would follow? Carolyne was his princess and he never wished that she had been a boy — a son — to take over the farm. She had proven herself to be every bit the farmer that any son could be. She still came home to help with the harvest. He thought of all the years they had walked the fields together. She knew every wet spot in the hay fields where you could get stuck in the early part of the year. And where the deer came to feed in the evening light. He'd shown her his favourite oak where he'd carved his initials and watched as she added her own. She loved the land but he had persuaded her to stay in school. What future was there for a girl, even his girl, on the farm? Now he seriously doubted the future for his farm. Oh there had been talk before, but it was only talk. Every year when the crops were small or the price of grain was low, the locals would sound off about the death of the family farm and yes, Florence was right, he had said on more than one occasion that there was no future in it, but it was just talk. Until his father died.

It was then, for the first time, that Tom stopped thinking like a steward of the land and started worrying about Tom Fisher. He had turned 60 that spring, and it had been like every other spring until the funeral. It was only then that he considered his age, and like many men when reflecting on time spent, he added up what he had made of himself. He pulled out some old school pictures. There was Mark, who had left the farm and got work driving a truck. He now owned a hundred rigs running into the States. And Barry, who never had much ambition but landed a government job in Regina. He took early retirement five years ago, with a good pension and full benefits. But it was Cliff's picture that Tom looked at the longest.

Cliff Anderson and Tom Fisher travelled to school together. Every day for nine years, for everyone knew that nine years of schooling was enough to work a farm. Besides, the local school only went to grade eight and one year of busing to town was enough. The Andersons own the farm next to the Fishers. Their grandfathers had moved to the area in a wave of migration lured by the promise of free land and the railroad. Cliff and Tom would stay on the land. While Mark and Barry and some other kids talked about leaving and finding work in the city, Cliff and Tom only ever talked about farming. When the others married and set up house in another town or even another province, Cliff and Tom just brought their brides home to their farms — the only homes they ever knew or wanted. To little bungalows just a stone's throw away. Tom still looks out the kitchen window, a hundred times a day, expecting to see his dad sitting on the steps.

In the eighth grade there was a girl named Thelma Dobson. Cliff and Tom both liked her but that's another story. Thelma's folks owned the farm to the south of the Fishers. Her dad got sick with something that today they call farmer's lung. His doctor told him he'd have to give up the farm. The place came up for sale and both boys went to ask their fathers if they would be in the bidding. Tom's dad listened to his son as they finished the chores. On the way back to the house he gave his answer:

"When your Grandpa and uncle Tom came here from England they each had a quarter section. It took them a dozen years to clear their land of trees and shrub. And you know we're still working on picking rocks. As my brothers and I got older and property became available we took on more land. Grandpa wanted to have a quarter to give to each of us boys. I took over the home quarter and after you were born and machinery got bigger your mom and I bought the other three quarters. It's not the biggest farm around, but Junior, it's plenty big for us. If we bought the Dobson place we'd have to borrow. And we couldn't farm 2 sections with our equipment so we'd have to go out and buy more, and borrow some more money. Besides, I'm sure there is some young family who's looking for a good farm. Some family that will make a good life here."

"But Dad, Cliff says his dad is talking about getting bigger. Says you can't stop growing or you go backwards. He says one day, with the right equipment, a man will be able to grow three or even four sections of grain."

"But why son? Why would anyone want to farm so much land? You'd be running day and night. And even if you could farm it all, would it really be farming? Would you have the time to walk the fields like we do now? Time to really know the land?"

Sure enough, Cliff's dad bought the Dobson place. A few years later they purchased a half section from the Stuarts and then the old Carmichael farm. When Cliff took over the reins from his dad he added several more properties until now there were 17 sections— that Tom knew of— that were under the Anderson Corporation. Cliff's brother is a partner in the fertilizer and lime plant and then there's the trucking company that the family owns. Cliff is a director on the boards of several public companies. Not bad for a kid with grade nine — same as Tom.

For the next forty-five years Tom would remind his dad of the missed opportunity. Every time the Andersons bought another block of land he would say: "It coulda been us, Dad." And every time they read a piece in the local paper about the Anderson empire he'd say: "They could be writing about the Fisher Corporation." But Tom senior never regretted his choice. Junior would go on about the huge four wheel drive Versatile tractors that were pulling 80 feet of cultivators, or the behemoth combines they had that could devour a quarter section field in one feeding. Then the older man would smile at his son and say something like:

"You know that mallard nest by the slough. I was by there this morning and the eggs have all hatched. Let's go down after supper and see how they're doing." And young Tom knew that his dad had made the right choice.

But the old man had died. He had died satisfied, after one final look at the field of barley. New life generated by the land, his land. If a man had to die, could there be any better time and place? But now — now when Tom was alone and mortal — he again looked at the picture of his school friend and thought "It coulda been us Dad".

It was this Tom Fisher that looked at his life as a small time farmer and grew anxious about his future. A few bad years and their savings had dwindled. For the first time that he could recall, the bank had called about their operating loan. He had cleared it up with the cheque from the crop insurance, but the Fishers didn't like owing money. He heard himself saying: I'm glad Dad's not here." He looked at others with their indexed pensions or million dollar corporations and worried that maybe he had failed. Failed to provide for their old age.

The television didn't help. You couldn't watch a news cast without being reminded of the plight of many seniors as the economy stumbles from one problem to the next. Scenes of grey haired grandmothers protesting the cut-backs to pharmacare. Social activists and opposition politicians uttering dire predictions of seniors being turffed out of nursing homes to become a burden to their children or fend for themselves. And the advertisers only added to Tom's feelings of failure.

Advertisers fell into two groups. One was showing you images of all your well heeled neighbours buying new products or taking exotic trips. The other was showing you how to become wealthy by buying into the lottery craze.

Tom couldn't remember when they bought their first lottery ticket. There had always been raffles for community and school projects — three tickets for a quarter— to win a patchwork quilt or a side of beef. But this was different. It was money, lots of money. And when the Reverend Ellery won $50,000 Tom had seen the lottery as a chance of ensuring their retirement. He bought most of his tickets at Harris' Red and White. It was the same store where the minister had bought his winner and his picture was still displayed above the ticket counter. Dressed in his clerical garb, he smiled serenely at each and every lottery purchaser. His hands were pressed together in a prayerful pose; the top half of the cheque stuck out above his fingers. Twice a week Florence and Tom ate their dinner in front of the television. She talked feverishly to Tom, to herself and to any unseen gods of good luck who could assist them like they must have done for the reverend.

"Can you imagine what it would be like to win the big one? Not the *real big one*. I've got no wish to have twenty million dollars Tom. Maybe five. That would be enough, right Tom? Remember the joke about the farmer who won the lottery and he said he was going to keep farming 'til it was all gone? We'd keep farming, right Tom? I mean no matter what, we'll stay on the farm? I wouldn't want to live anywhere else. And they all say you shouldn't change your life when you win. Of course we wouldn't dare keep it all for ourselves. There are so many good causes that could use our money. And Carolyne.. we could buy her a new house near Saskatoon. Close to the hospital. She's talked about nursing in the Saskatoon Hospital. Just a nice house in the city, so she could be handy."

Twice a week they watched the numbers come on the screen, finished their meal, cleaned the plates and discarded the slips of paper with the rest of the garbage. This modern concentration of gambling had turned into a major source of revenue for the government, but not for the Fishers. Tom and Florence were now spending $80 every month on lottery tickets. Their daughter Carolyne had studied addiction and was worried about her parents. She talked her mom into seeing a counsellor. When they learned that their lottery buying was actually slightly below average for people in Saskatchewan, Florence was relieved. Obviously they didn't have a problem if most people were spending more. All the same she and Tom tried to spend less. But it was hard to resist when the jackpot was 20 million and it only cost a few dollars to enter the dream.

It was cheaper than the semi-annual junket to Vegas. Tom called it a vacation but it wasn't a rest. And he never really saw much of Vegas. It was three or four days in a casino with a few thousand people, lots of noise, flashing lights and free food and drinks while you gambled. On the plane home they would swear off ever going again, but there was always someone who knew someone who had a cousin that had won big. Maybe the next time it would be Florence's turn to win at the slots. It could happen.

It hadn't happen on this trip. It had been the worst yet. Between Tom's losses at roulette and Florence feeding the slots they had managed to throw away $3,000. Tom was annoyed at his reckless squandering of their finances. "Even in farming you couldn't lose money that fast. Three thousand dollars would go along way to putting the crop in this year. What was I thinking? You won't catch me here again," he vowed as they boarded the flight to return home.

Well with all the snow they weren't quite home; but the stop over at the manor might just be worth the trip. In the wee hours of the morning, Tom and Florence talked at length of all that they had heard and seen earlier that evening. Could Randolph Webber III be their ticket to a secure retirement? He had suggested that they could be wealthy. Was there time? How much did they need?

It appeared that Michael Tibbet had very little and yet everything. And what of the Daliwahls? Their hosts lived on much less than their beautiful home would suggest. Appearances could be so deceiving. Just look at Jim Larsen. Who would have guessed that he was a millionaire? And he still had money worries. The more they talked the more questions popped up..... like dandelions in springtime.

By 2 a.m. Tom was trying his best to salvage a few hours sleep from the night. Florence was rehearsing a list of questions for the others in the morning.

"I wonder if Randolph will be down for breakfast? Do you suppose that woman is really his wife? I don't mind if she stays in her room until we're gone. Did you see the way she carried on? She was making eyes at you, Tom. And her no older than Carolyne. I never saw the like. Nope I don't care to see her at breakfast. There *will* be breakfast won't there, Tom? They do call this a bed and *breakfast* don't they? It sure is a nice place. It's hard to believe Bibi and Elizabeth don't have lots of money. What about the Hendersons? I wonder if the Hendersons would mind telling us how much money they have? Tom, how would you go about asking somebody about their money without sounding — you know — nosey? Tom? Tom are you listening?"

Tom was dreaming about breakfast. "Here Florence, have another waffle."

10

CHALLENGING THE EXPERTS

"An economist is an expert who will know tomorrow why the things he predicted yesterday didn't happen today.".... Laurence Peters

Charlie was reading in the parlour when Elizabeth came up from her temporary quarters. She poked her head through the doorway on her way to the kitchen, and was surprised to see any of the guests up so early.

"I'm an early riser," Charlie explained with a half truth. He was when Charles had something on his mind. He had been awake before dawn, methodically sorting and filing all the bits and pieces of data gleaned from yesterday's conversations. For the most part, he had been a quiet observer for it was in the observing that one gains knowledge. And knowledge was the tool that Charles would use to clear the path to retirement. It might even be the weapon to slay the dragon that held his savings captive.

When the first hint of morning crept into his

bedroom, slowly pulling back the night and revealing obscure shapes in the room, it came face to face with Charlie. He had heard the chimes of the mantle clock when he first woke and again, now striking twice to mark the half hour. But it hadn't been the clock that stirred him from sleep. It was Charles, anxious to put together a plan. Over the past few days, first at the library, then on the trip while Louise was driving, he had devoured the history of a hundred years of equity investing, and even more years of inflationary trends. He was a quick study and coupled with his existing information on interest rates, Charles had come to some firm conclusions. He was sure he was right. Of course, Charles was always sure he was right. "What's the point of having an opinion if you're not convinced it's right?" he would bluntly state to Louise whenever she questioned his dogmatic statements.

He intended to confront his Mr. Pattersen at the mill with this newly acquired knowledge. Pattersen had all the answers in their initial meeting. Charles had been silenced, and then won over to the financial planner's line of reasoning. Perhaps he would once again be able to refute Charles' information. After all, the market had been on a steep decline for the past three years. There must be a lot of unhappy people — people with questions. Any salesman worth his salt would be aware of the questions, and would need a response, something to calm the masses. Pattersen would be up for the challenge, for Charles knew him to be a talented salesman if nothing else. He thought back to that day at the mill — in front of all the guys that had looked to Charles for financial advice. He had been caught off guard. It wouldn't happen again.

His plan was simple. He would rehearse for this next

meeting using his fellow guests. This Randolph Webber was a good stand-in for Pattersen although he wasn't quite as smooth. He tried too hard and at times it became obvious. A real pro would never talk about how much money he paid for his wife's clothes. Come to think of it, Pattersen would never have a wife like Gwen.

"If he did he wouldn't take her out in public," Charlie interjected.

Not a *Pattersen*. But he would do. He would be aware of all the industry rebuttals for those demanding an accounting of the dismal performance from the money experts. All the pat answers and anecdotal stories for why you had to keep your money in their funds. He could hear Randolph even now. He was sure to have some warning examples of those who got out just before the last big surge in the market — and lived to regret it. He would be ready.

Charles would just be asking questions. He wasn't there to win an argument. He was scouting out the opposition. The real game would be played at the mill with Mr. Pattersen, Harry and the other guys. Yeah Randolph would do just fine for practice. But first Charles needed to make a call.

He slid out of bed and dressed in the dark from the pile on the chair. Louise would have something to say about his clothes when she came down, and he'd have to change, but that could wait. He fumbled quietly through the desk and found a phone book. With the directory and his note book of facts, he had made his way downstairs to the parlour.

There were some small dry pieces of maple to be added to the smouldering remains of last night's fire. He had hovered about until flames were rekindled and then added some blocks before settling into the deep leather armchair closest to the fireplace where he could enjoy the fire, keep an eye on the hallway, and continue to search the white pages.

He found a number and dialed ..... and apologized when he woke up the other party. He asked two brief questions, wrote down the responses, and went back to the directory looking for a name. Not there.... perhaps a different spelling. It could be unlisted. Did it even exist? It was at this point that Elizabeth stopped in on her way to the kitchen. Charles never took his eyes off the book. Several more attempts and he placed his finger below a name and address that might be the answer. He would call when the hour was more civilized.

Charlie's analytical half was reviewing his notes for the third time, when Badra and his two girls entered the parlour to greet him. Then the girls disappeared into the kitchen. Badra's eyes follow his children as if in fear that he should lose them again. "No," Charlie thought, "there is little chance for that to happen. He's much wiser now."

"We will need more wood," Badra commented and then, heeding his own words, he donned his parka and overshoes.

The fireplace — like all fireplaces — had no practical value, save for the rare power outage. Yet it was in regular use at the manor. The Daliwahls had long since come to terms with the economics of using it. It was inviting. The guests were drawn to it, and when the fire blazed it did keep the parlour warm. But with the chimney sucking up most of the heat along with the smoke, the wood's energy was wasted. To put in an insert would taint the old house, and so it was one concession to wastefulness that Bibi and Elizabeth were prepared to make. Charles agreed as he basked in its warmth.

Louise was the next to make an appearance. She made her way to the entrance of the kitchen where she stopped and inquired if she might assist. Louise was neither surprised nor offended by assurances from Elizabeth that no help was needed. Three in the kitchen — no matter the size — was more than enough. She joined Charlie in the parlour and was about to comment on his attire when they heard Florence.

Florence descended with an air of purpose. She gave a cursory look, then entered the room making inquiries about Randolph's whereabouts. "I've a couple of questions for Randy. He's quite something, isn't he Charlie?"

"Oh yes, he's something all right. I've a couple of questions for him myself, Mrs. Fisher."

"Imagine the good fortune of meeting such a man. And we have him all to ourselves. Do you suppose that it might be possible that Mr. Webber would take us all on as clients? We could meet back here — right in this very room — next year and we could all be rich. Not that some of us aren't loaded as it is. Did you ever see the likes of old Jim there? Who would have guessed?" Florence paused. She gave the Hendersons a closer look and redirected her inquiry. "Well what am I going on about? You and your missus never said too much yesterday except you live on Vancouver Island, you have two children — a boy Jason who is 23 and a girl Melanie 21 — you work at a pulp mill and your wife's folks live in Golden Prairie. You were awfully quiet. Tom says it's cause I don't give a fella much of a chance to talk, but I've never been with anyone all evening and still don't know anything about them. For all

anyone knows you might be loaded yerself Charlie.
....You're not, are you? You're not rich like Jim and
Randolph? Are you, Charlie?"

"Why Florence. Just yesterday, someone in this very
house, said I was a wealthy man."

Charlie shared a look with Louise, but managed to
keep a straight face. He delighted in the little awkward
dance that Florence performed as she struggled to excuse
herself while her blood pressure was showing its presence
in her face and in the enlarged veins in her neck.

∼

Tom had been up as early as Charlie. He had looked
out the bedroom window, surveyed the state of the weather,
and figured there was plenty of time to go back to bed. He
hadn't heard Florence when she went downstairs, but she
couldn't be ignored when she returned.

"It's not just Randolph and Jim that's millionaires.
The place is crawling with them. The Hendersons are
loaded too. He told me himself. *"Wealthy"* he says. Is that
more than a million Tom? How much is wealthy
nowadays?"

"I see you've managed to overcome your shyness
and ask a perfect stranger how much money he has," Tom
was shaking his head. It wasn't in disbelief. He'd long since
stopped disbelieving anything that Florence Fisher would
say or do. He wasn't angry or embarrassed, or any such
thing. This was Flo, and he loved her just the way she was.
She couldn't help being interested in folks. If the world was
full of more people interested in each other, would that be
so bad?

∼

Nobody was leaving early. The snow was still falling; the city remained motionless. The snow removal crews were all on stand by, for emergency calls only. They wouldn't report for work until the snow abated, and then it would take several hours for the main freeways to be cleared, several more hours for the lesser arteries to be freed. There was nothing to do but enjoy breakfast.

The call for breakfast brought everyone but Gwen to the dining room. Florence thought about her remarks last night and worried that perhaps Mrs. Webber was ill. "What if she died in her sleep and me saying such mean things about her?" she thought. She inquired of Randolph if his wife was all right and was assured that she was fine.

"She never gets up before ten," he said in a tone that Florence was unaccustomed to hearing. Tom would never speak about her in such a voice. She must have misunderstood the inflection in Mr. Webber's voice, for surely such a man who gave so freely of himself to help others, would never speak unkindly about his wife? Not that she approved of the way Gwen had flirted with every man in the house last night, but still.... On closer examination, Mr. Webber didn't look well this morning. There were dark shadows under his eyes — eyes that had as much red as the fire in the next room.

Tom looked at the table and thought of his dream last night. There were indeed waffles. Mounds of them, with whipped butter and an array of toppings of fruit jams, and of course maple syrup. And Elizabeth's fresh buttermilk biscuits.

Charlie was the first to finish breakfast. Bibi was right to boast about his wife's skills in the kitchen. While sipping on his third cup of coffee, Charlie reckoned it was as good a time as any to initiate his plan. Charles would need to stay on a leash . He was too aggressive, bounding off in all directions barking at anything that moved, he might scare off the prey. He would leave the questioning to Charlie.

"Listening to you yesterday, Mr. Webber, I got the impression that you're a man who knows his way around investments," Charlie baited.

"I've certainly made a lot of clients happy ....and rich over the years, if that's what you're saying?"

"Are they still happy?"

"What do you mean?"

"Given the sizeable drop in the value of equities I assume that your clients have lost money like everyone else. Do you think the stock market is a good place to have money invested at this time?"

"Charlie, I teach my clients early on in our relationship the importance of not getting emotionally involved in the market. There are always going to be swings in the stock market. But for the savvy investor, this is an advantage. When the emotional novice is panicking and selling I'm buying for my clients. I like buying when good quality investments go on sale. Wouldn't you, Charlie?"

"That depends."

"Depends on what?"

"It depends on whether these quality investments are still quality investments when the sale is over."

"Blue chip companies will always survive, Charlie. Look at history. You've always been better off in the equity market than in interest rates. You just need to forget about the moment and think long term. No one ever lost money when they stayed in for the long run."

"It's interesting that you should say that Randolph. Are you speaking from experience or personal research?"

"Both. I remember 1987. I started working for Discord Capital in 1985 and the market had steadily moved up. In the summer of 1987 I started advising my clients to take some profits. Sure enough the market fell in October. Most of my clients — those that took my advice— were sitting on piles of cash and were actively buying after the crash. In six months, the market was again making new highs. I tell you Charlie, we made out like bandits."

"Yes, I bet you did."

"Now this correction is lasting a little longer, but the results will be the same. As soon as the market gets rid of all the Nervous Nellies, it will carry on to new highs. It always has. Those who lose their money will have no one but themselves to blame for selling out at the bottom. There was this doctor back in `87. He was a big player but he never would listen. I tried to get him to take some profits but he wanted a little more. You know what we say about pigs in the market?"

"What *do* you say?"

"Oh it's a little saying the pros have. 'Bulls make money. Bears make money. Pigs get slaughtered!' So this doctor, he's leveraged up to his eyeballs when black Monday strikes. He should have been sitting with cash, but he hadn't listened. So now I'm telling him to ride it out. 'It's at the bottom. Hang on and you'll be all right,' I told him. But again, he wouldn't listen. Sold everything and took a bath. Of course a few weeks later and the market rebounded, like nothing ever happened, but it was too late for the good doctor. I tried to tell him, but he wouldn't listen. Doctors are lousy investors."

"But your clients are mostly in cash now. I mean you probably had them sell — take profits you called it — before this market came down, like you did before."

"Most of them. Not everyone listens — there are alot of doctors out there," Randolph allows himself a quiet chuckle before he continues in a more serious tone. "And I'll be honest with you, Charlie, few of us knew that the market would fall *this far*. How could we? How could anyone predict nine-eleven and a war on terrorism?"

"Honesty..." Charlie let the word linger on the end of his tongue. "Randolph, I like that in a professional. And your research?"

Research?

"Yes, you said that you were speaking from experience... and research. I wondered where someone might do some research on the stock market to come up with your statements about the superior returns over interest rates and the safety of blue chip equities?"

Well it's ...... it's all around you man!" Randolph Webber was between amusement and frustration with Charlie's seeming lack of sophistication. "Now I don't expect you to have the time or resources to attend all the seminars, lectures, and workshops that I have; but even for laymen there are numerous investing books that you can read."

"Books..... written by investment sales...uh consultants like yourself?"

"I haven't written a book yet. Not that I haven't been asked."

"And the seminars and lectures that you attend, are they sponsored by your firm?"

"Some are. It's part of a continual educational

process..... like doctors, accountants, and lawyers have. Creative Capital is at the forefront of professional development. We are always upgrading our skills. We have our finger on the pulse of the market and..." he paused to allow all those listening to grasp the importance of his next comment. "we have access to all the big boys in the market."

Charlie joined the others in gushing with admiration. Louise was onto his game, and nudged him when she thought he was sounding too much like Florence. He wasn't finished. "Oh I see. So a lot of your research comes from uh ...these big boys in the market. The analysts and executives from the mutual fund managers and corporate executives of blue chip companies. It must be pretty impressive stuff, being able to talk one on one with these important people?"

"Oh it's just part of the job. We're all professionals," he crowed. "We share ideas and information. But to be truthful, it's helping people that really gets me excited about what I do. Did I tell you about Carol Wicker?"

"You mean Charlotte Wicker?"

"Uh...yes Charlotte," Randolph sputtered as his face reddened. "Did I say Carol? I was thinking of Carol Adams, another wealthy client.

Good recovery, Charlie thought.

"Yes, I guess I did tell you about Charlotte."

"You know Mr. Webber, I've been doing a little research of my own into the stock market. You see I have some mutual funds in my retirement plans and, unfortunately, I didn't have a professional such as yourself to advise me to sell before the markets began to go down. I've been trying to decide what to do, so you can imagine my excitement when I discovered that someone such as yourself is right here ...."

"Why that's just what I was telling Tom," Florence

had taken a deep breath and Charlie knew he would have to wait. There was no competing with Florence. 'Tom,' I said. 'it's a miracle that Randolph Webber is right here among us. It's like a sign,' I said. Didn't I Tom? I heard the Reverend got a sign when he bought that lucky ticket. Did I tell you about our preacher winning the lottery for $50,000? Now I was wondering, Randolph, about how much money would we need to start with, so as we could be rich in four or five years? I don't mean rich like that other fellow who won the 649 for twenty million. Lord knows we don't want that much. Not twenty million. Just a little rich so we could retire like your other clients. We couldn't invest as much as some other people in this room," and she gave Charlie a vigorous elbow in the side, "but we have some money put aside. Don't pay any mind to what Tom says. That's just farmer talk. They're always crying poor. Don't let that stop you from taking us on as clients Mr. Webber. We'll come up with some money. Just tell us how much."

"Well Florence that is why you and Tom really need to have a long interview with me in the future. Then we can answer all of your questions. You need to get in touch with my office and set up an appointment." Randolph wanted to be free of this dirt farmer and his tiresome wife. Free to pursue the other guest that had more money to invest.

"Now Mr. Henderson you had some questions. Perhaps we should discuss these matters in private. The three of us?"

"Oh no! I wouldn't discuss anything without Tom," Florence bounced back in.

"I was thinking of Mr. and Mrs. Henderson," Randolph curtly explained.

"Oh there's no need for privacy, Randolph. My questions are not all that personal. I just need someone knowledgeable, like yourself, to check my research, to make sure I've got my information right. I'm afraid that I couldn't possibly come all the way to Calgary for an interview. And even if I was lucky enough to have you take me on as a client, I live on Vancouver Island. Remember? I don't see how it would be feasible to have an advisor so far away."

"No problem Charlie," Randolph was scrambling. "I have clients all across Canada. I could see you on one of my many trips to the west coast."

"*If* you were taking on new clients and *I* qualified?"

"Yes. Of course, I'm speaking only hypothetically."

"Could Tom and I be your clients hypothetically too Mr. Webber?"

"Sure Florence," his eyes rolling. "Go ahead Charlie. How can I help you with your research?" Randolph knew when to stop the chase. The best he could do was answer a few questions, impress this blue collar worker with his intelligence, and close the sale at another time. Away from Florence Fisher.

~

"Now I may sound like a *Nervous Nellie,* but give me all the reasons for staying invested, when every time I look at my statement I've got less money than the previous month. I don't even want to open the envelope."

"Okay Charlie. I'm going to take it one reason at a time, and real slow.

"Number One: History shows that you can't afford

to be anywhere else but in equities. Over the past 50 years the market has been up 70% of the time and bull markets — that's when the stock market has been strong — have lasted 4 times as long as bear markets, or when the markets have gone down."

"Randolph, bears are strong too! Why one time over at the Hicks' place a big bear mauled a bull so bad they had to put it down. Didn't they Tom?"

"Yes Mrs. Fisher. I'm sure bears are strong too. And I'm sorry to hear about the Hicks' bull. Look, it's just names that are given to different periods in the stock market. Okay? Sometimes we say it's a bear; sometimes the market throws stocks higher like a bull with horns. May I go on?"

"And you're saying 70% of the market is bull?" Jim's humour was alive and well. He figured that he was entitled to add to any discussion about the market. After all, he was the fellow sitting on 60,000 shares of TransAlta. Besides, he never fully trusted anyone in a suit and tie; but they were always good to have a little fun with. You take a good kid and put a suit and tie on him, and suddenly he gets right serious and thinks his work is so important. Jim didn't look it, but he had done some reading and he'd come across a quote by Bertrand Russell that he'd committed to memory: 'One of the symptoms of an approaching nervous breakdown is the belief that one's work is terribly important.' Jim had made a lifetime practice of helping folks who suffered from this symptom.

"That's not exactly how I said it. A bull market is defined as anytime the indices or groups of specific shares rise by more than 20%. A bear market is the reverse; when these same shares go down by more than 20%. Now, what

I was saying Charlie, is that over the past 50 years there have been 13 bull and bear markets. The bull markets last an average of 26 months and the market gains over 75 %, while the bear markets last an average of 18 months and only give back an average of 27%. So to any reasonable person," and he deliberately turned away from Florence, "any reasonable person can see that the equity market is the best place to invest your money."

"And the next reason Mr. Webber?" Charlie was meticulously taking notes of each point Randolph was making.

Randolph watched appreciatively and thought, "At least my words aren't being wasted on Charlie Henderson."

"**Number Two**: If your not in equities, inflation will wipe out all your gains in fixed income like GICs, T-bills, and bonds. Inflation is always close to the rate of interest that you receive. After you pay tax on your interest income, you're actually behind. Have you got all that Charlie?"

"Actually fall behind inflation," Charlie read from his notes before asking: "And this inflation is a big factor in our retirement?"

"Oh absolutely. I don't expect you to comprehend all the details but just think of it this way. When inflation is at 4%, every 18 years prices double. The loaf of bread that costs $2.50 today when you are .... how old Charlie?

"Fifty-three."

"The bread that costs $2.50 today when you're fifty-three, will cost $5.00 when you're 71 and $10.00 when you're 89. You can figure out for yourself what a car or a house will cost. Inflation isn't so bad when you're still working, because wages go up as well. But what are you going to do when you're 89, Charlie, and bread costs ten bucks and a new car is a hundred grand?"

"He won't need a car to go to the bakery, because he can't afford the bread!" It was Jim again.

"And us farmers will still be getting the same price for our grain," Tom muttered.

"Bread costs ten dollars when I'm 89" Charlie scribbles.

"Number Three: Taxation. The profits you make and the dividends you receive from Canadian shares are taxed much less than the interest you get from GICs and Bonds. If you make $10,000 profit on a mutual fund, you probably will pay no tax. Try doing that with a Canada Savings Bond. You'll lose almost half to the government!" There is unanimous agreement in the room on paying less tax. 'No tax on profits' Charlie enters under the number 3.

"Number Four: You should be happy that the market is down now. You can buy so many good stocks and equity funds at bargain prices. Remember my clients of `87? Now's the time to buy Charlie."

"Buy more?"

"Yes Charlie. Buy more at reduced prices. Average down. You'll thank me in the years ahead. There may never be another opportunity to buy at these prices," Randolph stares as Charlie writes in bold letters **BUY NOW!,** and his face brightens.

"Number Five: and this is probably the most important lesson, Charlie. You need two pros on your side. A professional money manager who has all the right information to buy quality stocks at the right time and add them to your fund. And a pro, like me, who will keep you on track and focused on your goal of a rich retirement. With a diversified portfolio the risk is minimized, and the longer you're involved the lower the risk. Remember this Charlie: 'It's not timing the market that will make you rich it's time in the market.' Write that down." He pauses while his student complies. "And don't forget: I'm always here, monitoring your portfolio, advising when to buy and sell, when to take profits and buy back in at a lower price. It's teamwork Charlie; and we're going to make a great team."

"You mean hypothetically? *If* you were to take me on as a client?"

"I've got a good feeling about you, Charlie. Can't you feel the chemistry?"

"Your chemistry is one part fresh biscuits and three parts my rum from last night," Jim's a natural with the one-liners. Charlie is thinking of bringing him to his meeting with Mr. Pattersen. "In a few hours all that chemistry will be making its way down the Bow River."

Randolph is determined to ignore the interruptions and presses on. "I know you're nervous and may find it difficult to hang in, and that's precisely why you need me. I've seen dozens of corrections and hundreds of nervous investors, and believe me Charlie, you'll be a winner if you hang in."

"But it's not without risk," Charlie reminds him. "Especially now. The market is all over the map. Why shouldn't I get out for the time being, and come back when things stabilize a bit?"

"This is the time to be *in* Charlie. When all the amateurs are rushing for the exit, the smart money enters.

Now, it would have been better if you had sold at the top —
like some of my clients — and were getting back in at these
bargain prices, but seeing as I wasn't there to advice you...
Well let's just say that you can chalk it up to experience and
I'll be with you the next time when it's time to take some
profits. But for now, think about this: What day is the
market suddenly going to shrug off the bear and start
climbing? Do you know? No one does, and that's why you
need to be there every day. Here's something for your
research: 60 % of all the gains in the stock market over the
past hundred years were made in just 20% of the time. If
you were out of the market just 20 % of the time — that's
one day a week — you could have missed out on 60% of the
growth.

  "Rational people are prepared to take a small
calculated risk, if the reward is sufficient. Charlie, suppose
you're standing on the corner of a deserted street. You see
a hundred dollar bill lying on the street. There are no cars
around. Would you risk leaving the safety of the corner and
venturing out to get the $100."

  "Go for it Charlie!" yells Florence.

  "And this has something to do with owning mutual
funds?"

  "Definitely. The opportunity to make some real
money is there. There's a small calculated risk... but look at
the reward Charlie. You just need to step away from the
corner. There's always the possibility that a car will come
around the corner, but you keep your eyes open, and
Charlie, I'm right there with you, watching."

  "What about all the dead guys lying in the street?"

  "Dead guys? There are no dead guys."

  "Sure. Look for yourself."

"There are no dead guys," Randolph raises his voice. "What are you talking about?"

"Over the past three years, everyone who has reached for that easy money has been run over. It's hard to see the cars, but there's no mistaking all the dead bodies. The money experts have been coaching us ordinary investors back into the market ever since it started to fall, and so far, it has been financial carnage."

"But the market won't stay down much longer. Bears never hang around for long."

"I remember this ol bear...." Florence began.

"Another biscuit Flo?" Tom handed her one without waiting for a response.

"What if the market doesn't recover for some time? Remember 1929? I keep hearing all this reassurance that you can't lose over the long haul, but look what happened after 1929. It wasn't until 1955 that the market recovered to the same level that it was in '29. That's twenty-six years Randolph, and a long time in anyone's life."

"Charlie, now we're much more sophisticated investors. A hundred years ago people were superstitious and easily spooked. People used to carry around a rabbit's foot, or hang horseshoes over the door. Today we have computer buy programs, intelligent, educated, and highly trained analysts. I've personally completed an exhaustive four year study program for my CFP."

"So you don't subscribe to all the market theories, like the change in the length of skirts determining the rise or fall in the market or who wins the super bowl? And horoscopes, are they better than horseshoes?"

Randolph was hoping Charlie hadn't heard of all the wild ideas for predicting the yearly antics of the most widely followed concentration of capital in the world. "Nobody really believes that stuff. It's just a diversion from the serious work of making our clients rich."

"Where were all these sophisticated people when my mutual fund was loaded up with Nortel and JDS? My fund was buying Nortel all the way down to ten bucks. Then they were embarrassed to have the stock show up in their portfolio and dumped it as it fell below a dollar. Now they own none at four dollars. At the height of the high tech craze the average growth fund had 29% of their money in high tech stocks. Now these same experts are saying that they knew all along that these stocks were over priced." Charles was off his leash.

"I'm sure glad to hear that the markets will be moving up any minute now because bear markets don't last all that long. The average mutual fund has given back any gains it made in the late nineties and the five year average return is at or near zero. Many of my co-workers actually think they're still ahead, but they forget that they've been adding more capital every year. The reality is we've lost money — and time. The 3 percent that I was guaranteed in GICs before my discussion with another financial planner looks pretty good by comparison.

"But I've got a question for you, Randolph. If the stock markets can't stay down as long as they did a generation ago, what's happening in Japan? The Nikkei Index started falling in 1987 and is still going down. Sixteen years later, it's only worth one quarter of what it was then. Are you saying that the Japanese are not as sophisticated as we are? Why were we sending our brightest young executives over there in the eighties to copy their business models?"

~

THE AMAZING DOW

For the first time in two days, Randolph Webber has nothing to say. Charles had startled him with his forceful comments.

"Slow down Charles, I'm to ask the questions," reminded Charlie. "You can explain the chart. Calmly."

Charles would be all right, now. He was narrating history. He opens his note book and pulls out a visual historical chart of the Dow Jones Index. Unfolded and spread on the table, it chronicles the unsteady path of the North American economy as companies and shareholders struggle to grasp the American Dream. Charles had made copious notes along the jagged line that formed the graph. All eyes were focused on the chart as he pointed out milestones in America's past hundred years.

President William McKinley's assassination produced barely a hiccup; easily overshadowed by the San Francisco earthquake. The sinking of the Titanic was actually followed by a small rally, as was the revolution in Russia. After 30 years the Dow had reached 160 points a four fold gain from its beginning.

"That's an average yield of four and a half percent. If you add in dividends the annual return was closer to seven percent," says Charles. "Interest rates were about three percent during this time. The companies making up the Dow had names like Allied Chemical, Sears, General Motors and General Electric."

"I told you, Charlie. Quality companies. You can't lose with companies like that. You just need to stick with them." Randolph was feeling a little better.

"I must admit, Randolph, that 7% is a pretty good return and that's about what the Dow has given over the past 105 years when you add in the dividends. Is that the way you see it?"

"We agree on that Charlie. But you know, I think you and I can do even better, with a little help from some money managers that I'm connected with."

"Better than The Dow? That would be impressive. Over 80% of money managers return less than the indices over a ten year period. Why do you suppose that is, Randolph? I mean apart from the high fees associated with mutual funds."

Randolph was feeling a little squeamish again. "Well I'm sure .... I mean 7% ... uhh some of the brochures that I have show ten and twelve percent gains. And commissions are negotiable you know."

"I'm afraid your brochures need some updating. They might have been accurate for a few funds during a select period of the nineties, but your own industry shows that most funds fail to perform as well as the Dow, and that's before expenses. The expenses of owning mutual funds are not the commissions, but the ongoing management expense ratio. On the rare occasion that the mutual funds surpass the performance of the Dow, fund managers boast with glee and scurry off to collect handsome bonuses attached to such a feat. The reality is that few mutual funds consistently perform as well as the Dow — in good times or bad. That's why the index funds that mirror the Dow and other indices have become popular, and you surely don't need to pay a money manager to have a computer buy stocks to imitate the Dow.

"How is that possible? I mean you've got scores of money experts, tripping over reams of reports, feeding every possible tidbit of information into computers for instant analysis on every publicly traded company around the globe. Surely they can do as well as 30 stodgy blue chip veterans. If they can't beat The Dow, why are they being paid big salaries at the expense of every mutual fund holder?" He spoke as much to the others as to Randolph. The roles had been reversed. It was Charles who was educating. His students had no answer, so he carried on.

"The reason is simple. **The Dow cheats**. If you think that's an exaggeration consider this illustration borrowed from every market pundit ever to be asked about investing: **"The Long Run"**. Yes, every time a client asks: "Why am I losing money?" the financial planner talks about the long run. Every time an analyst is questioned about his latest recommendation that went sour, he pulls out 'the long run'. It goes like this:

"Investing is not a get-rich-quick scheme where you sprint your way to easy wealth. No, investing is more like a marathon, where a well prepared runner paces himself. Along the way there will be obstacles that may slow you down or even cause you to detour momentarily. But if you stay the course you'll succeed in the long run. You can hear the music as the chorus is repeated ... 'IN THE LONG RUN.'

"Can you see yourself? You're at the starting line of The Boston Marathon. You've practiced for months. You've shed twenty pounds and most of your clothes. You're doing stretches while you wait for the signal. You're there with thousands of other hopefuls; each runner distinguished by his name and number on his shirt. You have your eyes fixed on Joe Dow. He's the one to beat — the record holder. You start out, quickly at first, to get ahead of the crowds, and then into a steady calculated pace. For the first 100 meters you run stride for stride with Joe, but his speed increases and you're content to let him lead. It's impossible for him to continue at that pace. He'll be forced to slow down or he'll burn out.

  "After two kilometers Joe has out-distanced all other competitors. He's barely visible but it appears that he has stopped and is talking to someone on the sidelines. There's an exchange of shirts and a runner takes off. He's wearing the Dow label. It's the last you see of the pace-setter. Joe Dow sets a new record. He grabs the headlines and inspires thousands more to enter for 'the long run'. If you investigate, you will learn that twenty runners ran a relay with the same name, 'Dow', while thousands of others staggered through a marathon. That story is never reported in the press.

  "Like our race winner, *The Dow* is not the same participant that was introduced to the public in 1897. Not the same competitor that sprinted into 1929. Not the same as the Dow following the Second World War, or the Vietnam War, or even the Gulf War. The Dow stocks have really been running short relays while advertising impressive results 'for the long run'. Like our Joe Dow, when the Dow stocks get tired or stumble, the index just replaces them with a new sprinter that can impressively cross the finish line. Yes, Randolph, there were and still are stellar performers like General Electric and Eastman Kodak. By the way, these are the only two stocks in the history of the Dow that have done better than the average 7%. But what about the others? There's no sense in being held back by has-beens like Johns-Manville and Union Carbide. Dow stocks like Woolworth, Anaconda, and

Bethlehem Steel are not even a distant memory. Unless of course you owned them. You don't have the option of adding only the winners, while quietly discarding losers. Not when you're holding on for the long run.

"If you look at the 30 stocks that make up the current Dow roster you will see that the switching continues. Microsoft and Intel, Home Depot and Wal-Mart have recently replace the tired and ailing, with the fresh and healthy. In fact, there's evidence that the time a stock remains in the Dow is being reduced as companies shine brightly for a few years and then quickly fade."

"Or worse — crash and burn!" says Jim. Charles looks at Jim and concludes that all his stock picks haven't been as successful as TransAlta.

"But you can't dispute the terrific returns of the nineties. Where else could you have made 15 to 20% a year? And I'm talking after expenses, Charlie. I know. I was there!" For the first time that he could remember, Randolph wasn't selling. He might not win over Charlie but he believed in the stock market and felt duty bound to defend it. He really hadn't considered the past history. He just repeated what he'd been trained to say. But the eighties and nineties, those were his years and he knew he was on firm ground.

"Yes Randolph, those were good years. Unprecedented years — maybe never to be repeated. Look at the charts. In just 18 years, starting in 1982, the Dow Jones Average charged from 880 to almost 12000. That's about 16% a year — just like you said Randolph. But to understand the market you have to ask: Why?"

"Why?" The question echoed around the table as each uttered the word. Some were repeating the question. Some were asking: "Why ask why?"

"Naturally we want to know what to look for so that we can take advantage of the next long bull market. So we need to know why such a growth in the stock market occurred. What do you think caused it Randolph?"

"The market moves when the economy is growing and GNP is strong."

"Good answer. But I don't think the right one. You see in the preceding eighteen years — from 1964-1982 the economy grew by twice the 1982-2000 rate and yet the stock market never moved. See the chart. In 1964 the Dow Jones was almost 900. That's the same as it was at the beginning of the bull market in 1982."

"So Charlie, what's the answer?"

"Did anyone here have a mortgage in 1981?"

"Yes I still remember. The interest rate shot up to 21%. Our mortgage was very small, so we could pay, but many of our friends lost their homes," Bibi recalls with a degree of sadness.

"In 1962 the mortgage rate was 6% and inflation was about 2%. With the increasing cost of the Vietnam War and then the oil crisis in the 1970's inflation soared, and so did interest rates. Even with increased production, the stock market had a hard time convincing the public to invest. With inflation, there is an urgency to buy an item before it goes higher in price. That leaves little money to invest, and if you have savings and bonds that are paying 17% guaranteed, why would you risk it in the stock market?

"Interest rates peaked in the early eighties. As they started to come down, and inflation was brought under control, companies started to attract investors. Now with interest rates lower than stock market returns for the first time in years, that pent up demand for investing was unleashed. The only real difference was interest rates."

"What about future inflation? Don't forget about inflation," Randolph insisted. "You'll fall behind with inflation and taxes if you don't invest. Have you heard about that, Charlie?"

"Yes Randolph, I have. That was your second reason to stay in the market, and I've heard it before," Charles would never forget that fateful encounter with Mr. Pattersen. "I want to ask you about that in a minute. But let's carry this present thought to a conclusion. So you have no growth in the Dow Jones from 1964 to 1982 as interest rates climb from 6% to 21%. Then you have an explosion on the upside in the market, as rates fall from 21% to .... where are they now?"

"The credit union holds my little mortgage at five and a half percent," Michael contributes.

"Five and a half. So where do we go from here? Any guesses?"

"Well, interest rates can't go down much further," Tom begins. "So I reckon sooner or later they're on their way up. And that there stock market of yours, Randy, is gonna be as worthless as rat droppings in a granary. Just look at the chart, Flo. Imagine having our money tied up for twenty years and making nothing on it. I might as well stay farming."

"Imagine having your money tied up in Japan for almost twenty years and losing three quarters of it," Badra remarks. "And I know that it can happen. I lost all my money, and I had control of the company. Businesses go broke every day — even big businesses — and the shareholders lose everything."

"And banks can go broke and savings accounts are worthless."

"Not really, Randolph. Deposits are guaranteed for

$100,000. It's the *shareholders* of the failed bank that lose," Charles was surprised that Randolph had made such a comment. Pattersen wouldn't be so easy.

INFLATION: SMOKE & MIRRORS

"Now, Randolph made a point about inflation as a reason to stay invested. And my research agrees with his statement, to a point. If you could consistently earn a 7% annual return in the stock market, you would outpace inflation in most years. But that's a pretty big *if*. But what if — instead of trying to run ahead of, or away from, inflation — we stopped and had a good look at this monster. Randolph, what is inflation?"

"I already explained it, Charlie. And you wrote it down. The loaf of bread ends up costing $10."

"Of course. And you're quite right. Inflation, according to the economic definition, is the result of too much money chasing too few commodities, resulting in a rising cost or a lower purchasing power of our money."

"Like trying to bargain for a good price on a hotel room, when there are none left in the city." Bibi offers. He's delighted with his choice of example.

"Exactly... I'm afraid," Charlie smiled, and then raised the question: "Bibi if hotel rooms were the only item that the government considered when they calculated inflation, and because of the storm the average room increased by 30% on the very day that the government calculated the increase, how much would the inflation rate be?"

"Why, 30% of course!"

"Now Tom; What if you stayed at home and never

used a hotel room. How much would inflation affect you?"

"Zero."

"Well almost zero," corrected Rick. "The ambulance driver that stayed in the motel was reimbursed by his company, and so their expenses went up. Six months later, their rates went up by a dollar. If you need an ambulance, the increase will affect you."

"And the airlines have extra expenses," Michael adds. "So if they're out of bankruptcy protection and still flying, when I take my next trip, the rates may be higher. But not 30% higher."

"So what I'm hearing is, inflation is a pretty subjective term. If you're not purchasing the item that's included in the basket of goods that measures inflation, your increase in living costs may be much different than the official number. Rather than look at the consumer price index (CPI) as an average, we should look at the items we will need in the future."

"I couldn't get along without bread," Florence confesses.

"Nor could I. But it doesn't bother me in the least how much tobacco products increase. A major portion of the CPI is based on housing costs and our needs in this area will be modest in the future."

"And all paid for," Louise states. "Except for the property taxes and they will be increasing."

"And you can forget about the $100,000 car. I don't have one now, and public transit works fine for me," Michael reminds everyone.

"Can you picture a retired couple, living quietly in a small place, surrounded by family and friends. They're not buying new furniture, or taking frequent exotic trips. They don't even eat as much, so that $10 loaf of bread lasts four times as long as the $2.50 one does now. Is inflation really such a scary thing?"

"Studies show that medical costs are rising far above the inflation rate. This must affect seniors," Randolph isn't conceding defeat.

"Yes it does. But it particularly affects affluent seniors. At least in Canada. Because, don't forget Randolph, we low income seniors will still fall under the government programs that provide many of the health care needs. I'm not saying that it won't have a negative impact, but it's pointless to worry about what may never happen. And it's even worse to take extra risks with your capital or squander your most important resource — time — in the hopes of scoring a big financial windfall, so that you can be prepared for every eventuality that may or may not occur."

"So you're just telling everyone to ignore inflation and it will go away. Isn't that a little irresponsible?"

"It would be if it was a real threat. I just don't think it is. And I believe history proves me right."

"Inflation is a fact of history," Randolph argues. "Thirty years ago a car cost $3,000. Now it's $30,000. That's a fact. That's history. That's inflation!"

"He's got a point Charlie. That truck I want is $45,000."

"I'm not disputing the fact that automobiles have increased dramatically. As have houses, and some other items. But don't forget, some things like television sets and computers have come down."

"And long distance calls and cellular phones," Badra's girls answer in unison. Leave it to teenagers to be familiar with that example.

"But I was really thinking of a little further out in history. You see we have a tendency to be fairly short sighted. History is more than ten or twenty years. Jim, what you see is that pick-up that you paid $5000 for twenty-five years ago. And now, when you go to replace it, the new one costs $45,000 and you figure at that same rate in another twenty-five years, the next one will cost $400,000. That calculates, but is it reasonable? In the 1930s there was a period in which prices came down because there was less money chasing an oversupply of products. The same thing is happening now in Japan. History indicates that these are not isolated incidents.

"Here's an example from history, Randolph. Two thousand years ago a labourer received a Roman denarius for a day's work. That is the equivalent of one Canadian dollar. That's about the same rate of pay that men were earning working for Andrew Carnegie in the steel mills at the turn of the last century. Over a span of nineteen hundred years there was no increase, no inflation. That's not to say that there were not pockets of inflation along the way but there were equal times of reduced prices. We have no way of knowing for sure which way prices will go over the next twenty years, but history is on the side of deflation — lower prices."

CAPITAL GAINS - CAPITAL LOSS

"You'll have to help me with this one, Randolph. Under point four I have a note that says I'll pay less tax with my money in the stock market."

"Yes. The gains are treated as capital gains or dividends. There's no tax on the first $100,000 of capital gains."

"But aren't you assuming a bit much? I mean I've been in these cursed mutual funds for the past two years and all I've succeeded in doing is losing 30% of our life savings." Louise's eyebrows go upon hearing the figure. "There's nothing to tax; capital gains, dividends or anything else," Charles was at it again.

"But you still *might* turn a profit — if you stay in," Randolph was no longer convinced that a profit was a sure thing.

"Okay. Say I stay in and in ten years time I'm still alive and these mutual funds are finally ahead, and I've got a profit. What difference does it make whether it's a dividend or interest or a capital gain that I show in my account?"

"Well the difference is you won't pay any tax if it's a capital gain."

"Really? It's in an RRSP. I thought all money was taxable when it comes out of an RRSP?"

"An RRSP? Well that's different. I was referring to accounts that aren't registered. *Then* you get a better tax treatment when you make a profit."

"But most of us have our savings in an RRSP, where you never get to use the preferred capital gains tax advantage. The capital gains tax exemption only applies to the few who invest outside their RRSP — *WHEN* and *IF* you make a profit."

"Well, yeah. Nobody expects to lose money. I mean, what would be the point of investing if you always lost money?"

"'Why?' indeed!. And what percentage of investors make a profit? Year after year. How many get to use this $100,000 tax advantage?"

"Oh I couldn't say. Maybe 70 or 80%..... in good years.... not the last couple of years.... Maybe a little less? Uhh... I really don't know. No one's ever showed me those figures."

"Well, I read a report on day traders that found that over 90% lost money and 70% lost *all* their money. Now, the statistics on investors would be different, but isn't it interesting that when you read about the super rich who have accumulated their wealth through stock market investing the name Buffett stands out. Do you know why?"

"Well the man's a legend. He's an example of the wealth created in the stock market."

"The reason that he's a legend is because he's the only billionaire to have made his money solely from investing. You've got billionaires who have earned their fortunes in software, in restaurants, in banking, shipping, the media, oil and real estate. You've even got a family of billionaires who made their money in mutual funds. *Selling* mutual funds! But despite the fact that over 50% of all American households own some sort of equities, Warren Buffett is the only man ever to become a billionaire by investing in publicly traded companies. He's a legend because he's so rare.

"So here's my point. Most people who are investing in the market are doing it in RRSPs, where you can't take advantage of the capital gains tax break, if they do manage to make a profit. Of those who are investing outside their RRSPs, many are losing money and because the loss is a capital loss, they can't even deduct that from their other earnings. So my point is, Randolph, don't you think your point number four about the capital gains tax break should really be a reason not to invest? I mean it seems to me that folks are losing their money in the stock market and then having to make up their losses from their other earnings that are fully taxed. No wonder the government was so willing to grant that tax concession. Tell me Randolph, have you ever claimed a stock market loss?"

"Well that's different. I'm a professional, so I have to claim all my trading profits as income."

"I was more interested in the losses. Surely even someone such as yourself, must suffer loses on occasion?"

"Tell me about it," Gwen had entered the room and was leaning against the doorway. "You might say *on every occasion.*"

"I don't always make money on my own trades," Randolph admitted, without acknowledging her. "I'm too busy helping others."

"Like Charlotte Wicker?"

"Yes. Charlotte Wicker and others."

"I took the liberty of calling Ms. Wicker early this morning," Charlie paused. "I wanted her comments on your work. You'll be pleased that she spoke highly of your abilities. She was telling me how she made over a thousand dollars in only three years. I had a little trouble finding her phone number. I remembered the area that you said she just moved to, and I called up an old friend of mine in real estate. He knew the person who had sold her and her husband the house. Her last name is Levine now. Dr. and Mrs John Levine."

11

THE PLANNER'S PLAN

"Try not to become a man
of success, but rather a man
of value.".... Albert Einstein

Randolph's embarrassment was interrupted by Tyler's entrance. He and his sister had been enjoying the snow; he entered the dining room covered in it. "Hey everybody! The plow just went by. You should see the piles of snow it made in front of the drive. Come and look! Oh yeah, there's a tow truck pulling out Mr. Webber's truck."

"Finally! Now I can get back to the office and a little bit of reality. Come on Gwen. Pack up, while I go and see the driver. He'd better not have damaged the Hummer," Randolph was reaching for his overcoat and rubbers as he spoke. He was relieved to be released from Charlie Henderson's barrage of questions and assertions. He had long ago lost control of the conversation. He looked up momentarily at Charlie and wondered if he had ever been in

control. He would think about that later. Now he needed to
deal with the Hummer. His call for roadside assistance had
never gotten through. Who had summoned a tow truck?

All but three of the others went to the living room
windows to watch Randolph wade through the snow and
ascend the banks that covered the entrance to the manor.
Bibi and Badra followed Randolph out the door preparing
to do battle with the mounds of snow that blocked escape to
the outside world.

Gwen returned to her room to pack. She wasn't
always as ready to follow instructions, but she was as
anxious as Randolph to leave, albeit for different reasons.
She had enjoyed watching him squirm, cornered by a group
of country hicks. He really was losing his touch. Not like
the man who had so impressed her with his fine clothes,
quick mind, and smooth words. He had showed her a good
time — in the past — when he had indulged her with
clothes, jewelry, and dining at the best restaurants. And
while there were still glimpses of the past in his spending on
her, Gwen knew the party was all but over. The mood
swings, the after-hours calls that set him on edge, the
hysteria he showed when she spent $300 getting her hair
done last week. It could only mean one thing. The money
was gone and Randolph Webber wouldn't be a lot of fun
without money.

He was in a hurry to get back and make some money.
She was anxious to look for a new ride and there wasn't
much to look at here. The old geezer had some money but
even she had standards, and besides, he would never spend
any money on her. No, there were others available. She
thought of all the men that she had met who had shown
interest in her flirtatious advances. Men introduced by

Randy. But that was of no consequence. It wasn't as if it was going to last forever. They lived in the big house together, but only strangers thought they were really married.

Had Gwen been watching Randolph, as were the others, she would have seen his animated conversation with the tow truck driver. She may have seen the paper given to Randolph as the truck drove off with the luxury SUV still in tow. Charlie saw it all — even the frustrated kick that Randolph landed on the side of the Hummer as it was hauled away.

"A most unusual way to treat a prized possession," Charlie thought.

"Unusual indeed," added Charles.

It took several minutes for him to return to the manor. Much longer than it had taken to leave. He stopped briefly to have a few words with Bibi before entering. He removed his coat and rubbers without a word, silently entered the parlour, and slumped into the big chair, seeking solace from the fire. The others left their window perches and made their way to join him. Randolph made no effort to conceal his worry, and although he had done little to endear himself to his fellow visitors, there was genuine concern for him – seasoned with a pinch of curiosity.

"More problems with your vehicle?" Elizabeth wondered.

"Uhh.. yeah, there's something wrong with it. It's not safe to drive so I sent it to my mechanic to get it fixed. We'll take a cab when they start running. It might be awhile."

"Enjoy the fire. You're welcome to stay as long as you need," Elizabeth's tone was as warm as the hearth. Randolph managed a faint smile.

"Charlie and I will be happy to drive you. We'll be leaving as soon as we're able."

"Sure, it's the least I can do after sounding off at you all morning. Look, Randolph, I hope you aren't upset with me phoning one of your clients. I know it might have looked a little sneaky on my part," Charlie looked at Louise to see if he had worded the apology correctly. Her eyes urged him further.

"And another thing: I had no right to trash the investment industry. I'm not saying I agree with the way they do business, but I shouldn't have said it in front of everyone. I don't really know you, but I'm sure you do a good job for your clients. Why even Mrs. Wickers ...or Levine said you were excellent. Anyway, I'm sorry, and I hope there are no hard feelings," Charlie moved closer and extended his hand. The gesture caught Randolph off guard and Charlie had almost withdrawn the offer before Randolph reciprocated. First with his hand, and then with words of his own.

"Thank you Charlie, but there is no need to apologize. I'm not sure yet of everything you said but I have a feeling you know what you're talking about. And if it needed to be said, well, it might as well be said to everyone. I'm afraid when you're selling there's the tendency to exaggerate the benefits, and overlook any problems. Maybe I've been selling this way for too long. I've even been selling myself. Trying to sell myself on the idea that things will get better. But they're not. I'm close to losing my job, I'm three months behind in my mortgage payments, and Elizabeth: my mechanic isn't fixing my vehicle. The bank is repossessing it. And Gwen and I ....well I won't even go there."

There was an awkward silence, while everyone assimilated this new Randolph. A humble, vulnerable — and very broke — Randolph. There was a slight cough from someone and two cleared their throats in an attempt to summon some words of encouragement. It was Tom who actually spoke.

"You need to talk to a farmer. We walk along the edge of bankruptcy all the time. Now the first thing you gotta do is know you've got a problem. Then you can make some changes and fix it. We used to have cattle as well as grow wheat. It just didn't work for us, so we got out of them. It works for others. Some guys have done real good with them. Still do. But it didn't work for us.

"How come a city guy like you has a big four by four anyhow?"

"It's part of the image. If you're successful you have these things. I meet clients, they see the Hummer and they figure if I can afford payments of $1500 a month then I must be doing something right. Some guys drive a Porsche or a Benz, but I'm the only guy in the office with a Hummer. The only guy who *had* a Hummer."

"I'm the only guy in my block who takes the bus," Michael announced. "Now that's *my* image. And does your image require a big house too?"

"Sure. It's just another piece of the package."

"So you have a lot of clients over?"

"I've had a few. None since the market has been down. Most of us are not doing much entertaining. We're watching expenses, and the clients that are calling ... well, let's just say I wouldn't want to be left in a room with a group of them."

"So why the big house? To show the neighbours that you're a success?"

"I've never met most of my neighbours. They're not home anymore than I am."

"Guys at the office? Friends?"

"Not since I first moved in."

"So help me understand this, Randolph. You live in this big house that's bleeding you dry, but you're never there, and nobody even sees it. You have to pay high property taxes, furnish it, heat it, maintain it, and have someone do the yard work while you help other people with their financial goals. Is that about right?"

"When you spell it out Michael, it does sound a little bizarre."

"Just how big a place do you and Gwen really need?

"We use the kitchen — once in awhile — a bedroom and bathroom. Gwen probably uses the family room; that's where the CD player and television are. I haven't been in some of the rooms for weeks. We really only need a two bedroom place.

"Real estate is pretty good right now, unlike the stock market. I could dump the place and come out with a bit of cash," Randolph was foreseeing life without the big house. Moving was no longer an admission of defeat, but a climbing out from under the burden of possessions that were robbing him of life. "I could use the money to pay off the bank and credit cards. We could rent an apartment for less than half of what the house is costing. No credit card and bank payments, a bus pass instead of the Hummer, I wouldn't need to make near as much money. Maybe if I didn't have to sell everyone I talked to, my job would start being fun again."

"And if you lose your job?" Elizabeth asks.

"Well, that's even more reason to get rid of the house. Isn't it? I've been panicking because I couldn't think of another job that would pay enough to cover all my bills. Without the bills, I'm no longer held hostage. I could take a page out of Rick's book and make less. I might even come and work for Tom and Florence. I was raised on a farm in Manitoba."

"No! You're havin fun with us!" Florence uttered in disbelief.

"Randolph Webber III doesn't sound like a name for a farm boy." doubted Tom.

"How about Billy Sawatzky?"

"Sawatzky? But what's all this Randolph Webber stuff?

"Afraid it's more of the image like the fancy car and the house. I figured the money people would rather give their money to Randolph Webber III than Billy Sawatzky, son of a pig farmer."

"I knew I could smell something, and it sure wasn't money," Gwen was standing in the hall with her suitcases. "Somebody call me a cab. This is where I say goodbye Randy — or should I say Billy. When you get back to the house put your stuff in another bedroom until I move out."

Elizabeth was quick to call Gwen a cab and when it arrived forty-five minutes later there was no shortage of offers to help her load her things. Bibi and Badra had cleared a path for the car to enter and turn around. When it pulled out there was a visible sigh of relief. They all rejoined Randolph in the parlour.

"Maybe she'll change her mind." Louise sought to comfort Randolph who had never moved from his chair.

"I hope not," Randolph made an attempt at humour. "Look, we're not married. Gwen never made any secret of the fact that her attraction to me had more to do with money than matrimony. She'd never be happy living in a two bedroom apartment. I couldn't afford her when I was making $200,000, and those years are over — right Charlie?"

"From where I'm standing it looks like a few lean years ahead. But other than you and I Randy, and maybe the Fishers, everyone here talks like Louise's folks. They're all for this living on less lifestyle."

"*Less money* Charlie. But *more* of the important things." Louise reminded him.

"I don't spend much," says Jim, "but I do love my million."

"Well my friend you should spend some money on a therapist." Michael's words elicited a round of laughter.

"You may love your money but she could care less about you." Tom repeats the lines of a Vegas stand-up act. "She's about the most fickle lover anyone ever had. Just when you think you're getting along fine — BAMM — she's gone. No explanation. First time you need a little help and she's nowhere to be found. Here you are, knocking yourself out for her, turn your back and she's over there with your best friend, snuggled up in his pants pocket. And have you seen the type of people she hangs out with? Not a farmer in the bunch. Not the type of folks you want to bring home. Low life...." Tom pauses looking for a response.

"You mean pimps and drug dealers?" Rick takes the bait.

"Yeah and bankers and barristers. So next time you're sweet-talking to your money Jim, just remember where she's been."

No comedian ever had a better audience. Who would expect Tom Fisher to take centre stage with Florence in the same room. Florence who had remained silent through it all waited for the applause to end, before she added a footnote.

"That's my Tom. After every trip to Vegas he mimics some performer. He usually saves it for our daughter so that she knows we saw something besides a roulette wheel and a slot machine. I'm so relieved. I thought he was going to impersonate Celine Dion."

"It's a good way to look at money," observed Randolph. "All my life I've wanted it. We were poor growing up, and I figured that the recipe to a better life had just one ingredient — money. I've made some money over the past ten years, and for a brief time I actually held onto a little of it. But even then I don't remember being all that happy. I spent most of my time trying to get more or worrying about losing what I had. I guess I was worried because I knew the easy money had to come to an end.

"Okay it's come to an end. And so has Randolph Webber the third. Now, how much money does Billy Sawatzky need to live on? Any good financial planners out there?"

"You're the one with the certificate, Randolph," said Charlie.

"Let's try *Billy*. I still answer to it when I go back to Manitoba. Oh, I passed the exams easy enough. But I need an apprenticeship. Some practical experience."

"We've all got plenty of that," says Charlie who acts as a moderator. "What's rent going to be for an apartment in the city?"

"I know what Raj pays for his one bedroom place," Elizabeth states. "It's $700. It's not downtown but there's a bus stop — and it's quiet. I think you can still get a place for seven or eight hundred a month."

"Okay. That's shelter. What about transportation?"

"You all know where I stand — or sit. On a bus. A bus pass is $65 for a year," Michael reminds the group one more time.

"That'll be great in thirty years Mike. But before I get a senior discount what will a monthly transit pass cost?"

"It depends on the zones but $85 a month should cover it," Ranjna informs the others.

"And for out of town trips you'll need to rent a car or take the Grey Hound. I'd double your budget to $170. Food?" Charlie asks.

"Pretty cheap if you eat at home and watch for sales," Louise counsels.

"Too cheap," whines Tom. "What other place on earth, or time in history, could a man with a decent job go to work and by Monday afternoon have made enough money to feed his family for the whole week? It's great for the consumer, but tough on us farmers."

"How much?" the late Randolph presses for a number.

"No more than $150 a month, once you have a few household items like paper towels and soap," Louise explains.

"Utilities?"

"Most apartments are heated but your electricity and telephone will cost $40 a month — if you're careful." Rick nods in agreement as Tammy relates their experience.

"Now you'll need things like tenant's insurance and personal items," advises Badra. "I budget almost $100 every month for such things."

"Your expenses so far are $1260 per month," Charles proclaims. "Have we missed anything?"

"We're not finished.... are we? Did anyone mention Flames or Stampeder tickets? How about a night out or even cable?" There's a little Randolph left in Billy.

"And there is medicare premiums, dental bills, and life and disability insurance," Rick reminds the group.

"And taxes," sighs Charles.

"Details, details," drones Jim. We're talking necessities here Billy-boy. If you have some extra money and want to watch some overpaid athlete in tight pants run down a field carrying an inflated piece of pigskin, go for it. But do it with left over money. And since when is watching 200 channels of human misery an aid to finding happiness? As for medicare: yeah you better add $50 a month in your budget for that. The life insurance, who are you looking after when you're dead? From the looks of it, Gwen's no longer a dependent."

"Not mine. But watch out if she moves in with your cats."

"She wouldn't....." Jim stopped as he caught the joke and gave Bill a look of approval. This kid is all right once he loosens his tie, he thought. Then he continued: "You've got disability insurance through work and if you lose your job, well the insurance only pays if you can't work — not if there is no work; so forget about it. And dentists are all overrated. I haven't seen one in years," he concludes as he pops out his set of well worn dentures.

"The beauty of making less money, Charlie, is that you pay less tax — a lot less tax. Billy's expenses will be about $1500 a month," Elizabeth said matter-of-factly. "That's almost the same as Bibi and I earn but then we own the manor and don't need to pay rent. We pay almost no income tax on that amount. For a single person, I would guess that you'll need to budget about a hundred to a hundred and fifty a month for taxes and other deductions."

"Unless you feel uncomfortable about paying so little tax." Louise reminds Billy of their animated conversation last evening. "Canada Customs and Revenue will only take what you owe, but if your conscience bothers you about not paying enough, the Feds have been known to accept donations. Of course you'll get a receipt and when you claim that it will further reduce your tax, and then you might feel worse."

"Okay, enough already! I get your point. I spend less, earn less, and pay less tax. Maybe I'll even get the GST rebate. Charlie, your wife has a mean streak. Haven't you told her about being a gracious victor?

"Fifteen hundred a month and a couple hundred for taxes and extras. Randolph Webber the third spilled that much a month but I think Billy might get along just fine." There's a look of relief on Billy Sawatzky's face when the simple truth surfaces. "I'll do it! And if Creative Capital lets me go, I'm sure there are plenty of jobs that I can do to make that much a month. We're talking a forty hour week at less than twelve bucks an hour."

"Or a twenty hour week at $22 per hour," Rick suggests. "That's my choice."

"And if you happen to find work outside the city — say on a farm in Saskatchewan," Tom pauses, "you can rent for a lot less. Why, you can buy a little place in our area for $50,000."

"You can buy half a town where I come from in Manitoba for $50,000," Billy exaggerates.

"I don't want to throw a wet blanket on this warm and fuzzy group," says Charles, as he takes a seat next to Louise, "but I do have a concern. I must admit that when Billy here was Randolph and complained about us — or some of us — not paying enough taxes, I could see his point. I don't mean that we should pay more than necessary, or even that it doesn't make perfect sense to earn less and therefore pay less tax.. But if everyone plays this game, where will the money come from to run all the senior programs that we're counting on — like subsidized nursing homes?"

"If everyone becomes a lawyer, who will operate on my hip when it needs replacing?"

"You want to explain that comment, Lou?"

"Sure Charlie. Just because a few of us here agree that life is more enjoyable if you focus a little less attention on careers and money, it doesn't mean we're going to change the world. There will always be those who are driven to make tons of money, regardless of the damaging side-effects."

"There's no shortage of those who love money and the things it can buy. Advertisers will make sure of that," adds Elizabeth. "And just as only a few of us may need our hips replaced, only a few of us will end up in nursing homes. You can't go through life worrying about every possibility."

"It's a fact that I pay far less income tax and receive more benefits than I did when I was working full time, Rick states. "but that's not a total loss to government revenue. Remember, Charlie, If I'm working three days a week driving courier, somebody else is working the rest of the week. Someone who was unemployed before; maybe drawing unemployment insurance payments or tapping into other social benefit programs. Now he's no longer drawing money from the government but actually paying into these programs. I often wonder what the unemployment rate would be if everyone worked four days a week instead of five."

"But surely it's irresponsible to shut our eyes to obvious future needs." Charles is not convinced.

"It's not only irresponsible but down right embarrassing," says Jim. "I knew last week I was low on gas. Of course if I'd bought it then, I would have missed all this fun."

"You are right Charlie, adds Rick. "But first you need to identify your future needs. For Tammy and I, our future needs were, and still are, those of our children. For us it would be irresponsible to shut our eyes to the need of spending time with Jessica and Tyler. We also have financial needs, but these can be cared for by working a couple days a week and keeping our wants within reason. At the same time we have a little savings and our house is paid for."

"But what happens if there's no Old Age Security?" Charles counters. "How will you survive?"

"That's what has us worried," says Tom. "We've got a little in retirement savings, but not enough if you listen to what the experts tell us."

"Don't forget about Canada Pension," Bibi reminds the group. "The Canada Pension plan is available at age 60, and despite the propaganda from special interest groups, it is very well funded."

"I mentioned my dad retiring next year, says Rick. "Ever since I can remember, he's been complaining about all the income tax he pays. Just wait until he starts drawing Canada Pension, his Old Age Security, his company pension and money from his retirement savings. He'll be yelling so loud I'll hear him when we're back in the Caribbean."

"Just a minute," interupts Billy. "You're not trying to tell us that he would have more money to spend if he didn't have any retirement savings?"

"Oh no. I figure he'll still get to spend about 40 cents of every dollar he takes from his RRSP. I just know how he's going to feel paying all that tax, and losing some benefits his neighbours will get because they have less income. He may even wonder why he worked all that extra time to be able to buy his RRSP. He'll get to spend some of it – unlike my friend with cancer – but he won't get to spend as much as the government gets."

"It sounds like your dad's income will be heavily taxed," agrees Charlie. "But if the government does away with Old Age Security and the Guaranteed Income Supplement, the only income that you're assured of, Rick, is Canada Pension, and that won't keep you."

"And Charlie," Louise begins, "what happens if the government seizes our RRSPs? It could happen. Some governments in other parts of the world have frozen bank accounts during an economic crisis. Of course we would be fine. We could always go live with my folks."

"A scary thought, Louise. But you're right. It's pointless lying awake worrying about the distant future. And we do have a good nest egg set aside –smaller than last year, thanks to the miracle of mutual funds, but judging from everything I've learned here, it will be plenty for our future needs.

"It will be if we get out of the market before we lose anymore. Did we really lose 30 percent of our savings?"

"Well Lou, it's not really lost until we sell." Charlie sheepishly repeats an old lie.

"Where did you put Charles? Charlie, stop talking nonsense and tell Charles we're getting back into GICs."

"I thought money didn't mean much to you. We'll be fine. Just look at your folks. Remember, that's what you are always telling me."

"I don't like seeing it wasted. Gambled away. And look what worrying about those mutual funds has done to you, Charlie. Even if we were making money with them they're not for you — not for us Charlie. Let's just tuck our savings back into something safe and guaranteed and make plans for retirement."

"Does that mean I can retire early, Lou?"

"Whenever you're ready, Charlie. There are always company buy outs being offered. Why not look into the next one?"

Together they listen to the other guests banter back and forth about growing up on farms or in small towns, the people and the weather. Always the weather. For the moment the weather had improved in Calgary. The sun had replaced the clouds and was quickly reducing the snow on the roof to streams of water cascading over the gutters that were still plugged with snow. Badra had finished blowing out the parking area. Michael and the Fishers waited for their shuttle to the airport. Charlie and Louise would take Jim to the nearest gas station and then run Billy home to begin putting his new financial plan in practice. They would then carry on and make the five hour trip in time for supper, a day late, but a day well spent, for even Charles was at peace. He knew now what lay ahead. No longer was he in doubt about his financial future.

Charles and Bill Sawatzky weren't the only guests who had made decisions about their future. Jim was tip toeing around an idea that involved the Fishers.

"You fella's wouldn't be needin a few rat catchers and their trainer would ya? I could bunk in that spare house on your place. My cats stayed in an old outbuilding `til the city said to tear it down. Calgary's smothering my place. I've been itchin to move and the neighbours wouldn't shed any tears. I used to look out over acres of prairie and listen to Coyotes. Now I'm looking into some guy's back yard and listening to them fighting, or complaining about my cats. I sure do miss the

coyotes. I hear tell there's plenty of em around your area --
that's if that ol bear ain't got em all, hey Mrs. Fisher?

"I don't have much spare cash but I could swap you
some TransAlta shares for it. I wouldn't hold onto `em for long
though, if Charlie's got his facts right."

"We got a barn that would hold a hundred cats. And it'd
be good to see someone in the bungalow. I don't think we'll be
needin` the money. Flo and I have been paying into Canada
Pension since day one. It's time we started taking some out.
Not that I'll quit farmin. Not as long as I can climb aboard a
tractor, walk the fields. I still love working the land. But I
could use another set of hands, come planting time.

"Sure thing, Jim. Come on out for a visit and bring your
cats. See how you like it. Any day now the mallards will be
back looking for a place to nest. I haven't been checking on
them the way we used to — my dad and I."

Tyler and Jessica are back inside, covered once again
with snow. Tyler is tugging at his dad as both youngsters plead
with their parents to join them. "We're making a fort. Come on
quick — before it's all melted!" There's little chance of that,
given that more than thirty inches of snow has descended on
the area in the past 24 hours. But to a child, a moment lost to
further conversation is unacceptable. They fully understand
the need to "seize the day". They see with clarity that a missed
opportunity is lost, never to be recovered. It is inconceivable to
postpone the building of snowmen, forts, or making snow
angels until the next snowfall, for perhaps this is the very last
snowflake ever to drift out of heaven's storehouse down to
planet earth.

Logic speaks of many more snowfalls; if not this spring
then surely next fall or winter. But to a child this is the time.
For they know instinctively — without logic — that play is

relegated to a few short years before it no longer becomes acceptable to flop in the snow for no reason other than because it's there. Before reason suppresses spontaneity and you need to consider consequences and ask advice and form committees to rule on every action. Oh, to be young.

"I'll go." Charlie says quietly.

"Go where?"replies Louise.

"I'll go with Tyler and Jessica." his voice is a little more sure.

"*Really,* Mr. Henderson?" Tyler is sizing up his new playmate. "You're kinda old. Is it all right with Mrs. Henderson?"

"Sure. I'll go play," Charlie's voice is strong and excited. "And Mrs. Henderson will come and even stuffy ol` Charles."

"Charlie, remember your back," Louise cautions.

"Everybody outside!" Charlie yells. "Come on Billy and Jimmy. Come on Bibi and Badra. Mikey and Tommy, you have time before your bus comes. Quick, before the snow's all gone!"

If the neighbours on 25th street had been at their windows, as neighbours are after such a storm, what a sight they would have witnessed. Children playing. Children in grown-up clothes. Big kids in leather top coats and parkas; in make-believe disguises to look like middle aged men and women with grey hair and extended stomachs, hunched backs and balding heads. Children flopping in the drifts of snow and rolling snowballs into massive building blocks for forts and snowmen with vigor and the wide eyed wonderment of youth.

When everyone was soaked to the skin and once again feeling their age, Charlie disappeared around back to where the Volvo was parked. He quickly returned with his childish grin still in tact and announced: "Look everbody! I have chocolate, lots of chocolate. He marched into the manor like the pied piper followed by ten staggering 'kids' of all shapes and sizes. Kids that stopped to wipe the mist off their bi-focals and sat down heavily to remove their foot wear. Off with their overcoats and rubbers and mittens. Elizabeth dug around in the pantry and hunted up a bag of marshmallows and the troop headed for the parlour and squatted in front of the fireplace. Marshmallows were roasted and pressed between chocolate covered waffers as they shared stories of former campfires and adventures as children. They hauled out memories yellowed with age, forgotten memories recalled while under the influence of large quantities of chocolate and marshmallows.

Forgotten were the discussions of The Dow Theories and dividends and strip bonds. There was no more talk of taxation, inflation, retirement income funds and indexed pensions; no worries over the medicare crisis or the state of the Canada Pension Plan and a thousand other grown-up topics that smother campfires and silence the giggles of youth. Forgotten, until the horn of the shuttle sounded, announcing the imminent departure of the Fishers and Michael Tibbet to resume their flights home. They left like reluctant children, dragged away by parents who have a schedule to keep.

And then it was Charlie and Louise's turn to say good-bye to their hosts. They took Jim to the nearest gas station and then brought him back to his truck.

"This will be the last drink I give to this old fella," Jim promised them. "Yep I figure on gettin me a new one first thing tomorrow – or as soon as I can sell some shares and get a cheque."

They followed through with their offer to Billy and drove him home to his big house in Quail Estates, an upper middle-class subdivision. Charlie asked him to keep in touch and let them know how he was making out with his new budget. "I never thought I would tell a investment salesman to keep in touch," he told Louise, as they were driving out past the security gate. The street turned onto Deerfoot Trail and in a few minutes they were on the Trans Canada heading east.

Louise called her folks to let them know that, yes, they were finally on their way and would be there in time for supper. "We're fine mom. Yes we had lots to eat where we stayed. Don't worry. The roads are clear now, and you know how careful Charlie is when he's driving. Charlie? Oh he's doing great. Wait till I tell you what he did this morning. Charlie, upset about the delay? Well Charles was a little cranky at first, but we haven't seen him all day. Come to think of it, he might be buried in the snow."

12

YOU CAN'T LIVE ON THAT!

"The art of living easily as to money
is to pitch your scale of living one
degree below your means.".... Sir Henry Taylor

There was no detailed budget of my personal income and expenses in Free Parking. Some of you phoned or e-mailed and wanted one. Many of the reporters who wrote stories about my lifestyle asked for one. And the odd talk show host challenged me for one.

The omission was intentional. The reason was simple. *Free Parking* was to be a book to stir up discussion and thinking about trading things for time, lifetime earnings for life and learning, finances for family. As soon as you attach a dollar figure to the equation, it becomes the focus of the discussion and too often stymies or kills further thought with an arbitrary: "You can't live on that!"

I misjudged my audience. Frankly, I wondered when I wrote *Free Parking,* if there *was* an audience. At the height of the stock market euphoria of the late 1990s and into March of 2000 there appeared to be little appetite for a voice in the wilderness crying: 'Earn less live more.' I was wrong. I realize now that by nature those who were already living a simpler life were doing just that: quietly going about enjoying time with those they cared about. They rarely make headlines. For these Canadians, and I discovered that there are tens of thousands of them, know all about budgets and living frugally.

Others were intrigued by the ideas in the story but not quite sure if I was for real and were my ideas sound. As the stock market collapsed and the high tech bubble burst, they were joined by a growing number of reluctant participants in the more simple lifestyle who also wanted to know if life does exist below the poverty line, since with no longer the high paying jobs or bulging portfolios, this would be their lot in life for the foreseeable future. They wanted some numbers. And I guess that's what I would want, if I was coming from their direction. So here are my numbers:

MY BUDGET
MONTHLY EXPENSES

Year	2003	2013
Shelter		
Interest on mortgage	250.00	
Insurance	50.00	30.00
Maintenance	100.00	20.00
Heat	100.00	30.00
Utilities	100.00	80.00
Taxes	100.00	60.00
Condo fees		120.00
Total Shelter	**700.00**	**340.00**
Food		
Groceries	400.00	300.00
Entertaining/Eating out	100.00	100.00
Transportation		
Gas	100.00	
Insurance	80.00	
Repairs/Replacement	170.00	
Public Transportation		20.00
Car Rental		100.00
Total Transportation	**350.00**	**120.00**
Clothes	100.00	50.00
Personal items/Gifts	50.00	50.00
Insurance	50.00	
Donations	50.00	100.00
Vacation	150.00	150.00
CPP/ income tax	100.00	50.00
Total Expenses	**2050.00**	**1260.00**
Company portion of expenses	(350.00)	
Actual Expenses	**1700.00**	**1260.00**

INCOME

	ACTUAL 2003	PROJECTED Age 65
Earned income	1400.00	
Interest income	200.00	200.00
My OAS		500.00
My CPP		400.00
Wife's Income	50.00	
Wife's OAS		500.00
Child Care Benefit	250.00	
Daughter's Income	50.00	
Total Income	**1950.00**	**1600.00**

Now before you poke holes in my budget with the: "Where's the money set aside for savings or emergencies?" and "What about this expense?" let me add a few accounting notes. If you read audited financial statements and budgets, be sure and look at the notes. That's the part where the author of the document explains any points that may cause you to misunderstand the numbers. It's also the part that gives the author a way out if the company gets into trouble in the future. So here are my **notes**:

Remember, this is my budget. It may not work for you or you may feel too nervous about not setting money aside every month for contingencies. To set your mind at ease I do have some savings as well as substantial equity in my business and our house. These assets will be used to buy a small condo and provide a small income when I officially retire at age 60.

I also have an almost unlimited line of credit from several banks, though, for the life of me, I can't understand why any sound financial institution would provide unsecured financing to a middle aged underemployed highschool dropout in the amount of one year's income. Wait, it get's even stranger. Not to be outdone, the other banks anted up to stay in the game and matched or bettered the first so that there are five of them that stand to be on the hook to the tune of $100,000 if every I should, in a state of dementia, take them up on their offers.

When I see the unsteady world economies and the breakdown in family life — a major contributor to personal bankruptcies — I somehow feel that easy credit will bring down a few more banks before things get better. I note that several of the banks that have been so liberal in offering me credit, have also reduced their provisions for bad loans thus enhancing their short term profit. If I were a betting man, which if you've read this far in the book you know that I'm not, I would lay odds that their bad loans will escalate causing them headaches in the near future. This will devastate their earnings. The stock should fall, making it a good short.

Come to think of it, if I drew down my line of credit issued by these banks, gave the money to my wife to short their stock, then defaulted on my loan and went public with the story; I could cause a run on the bank's stock, creating a windfall profit for my wife. She could then give me back the $100,000, I could belatedly pay back the banks and pocket the excess.

It was just a thought.

But I digress. Oh yes. So you see, you needn't worry. My budget works for me. There. Do you feel better? And yes, I know that changes the picture, and it may not be realistic for a young family just starting out in life to pay as little as we do for housing. or transportation. The main areas, where I see my budget differing from others at my stage in life, is in income taxes and money designated for retirement savings. While these two items make up a major commitment in many budgets, they hardly cause a ripple in my overall expenses. With little future needs for extra money apart from Canada Pension and Old Age Security, I need to generate much less income today, which in turn attracts very little income tax. How much less would you have to work if you paid minimal tax?

Is it irresponsible on my part to promote a less-income lifestyle? One journalist suggested that "some gullible readers could be persuaded to choose terminal poverty when they have the means to plan for a comfortable retirement." A fair comment except that the writer ignores the fact that I neither live in, nor promote, poverty. My family does live at or below the *official* poverty line but this is an arbitrary number that has little to do with reality. I have always planned for a comfortable retirement. I'm comfortable now, and I have no plans to change my financial situation when I retire.

And what of those who choose to retire with fabulous wealth? Before you dismiss this as an extreme desire held by only a jaded few, consider surveys that poll graduating MBAs who list as a primary goal, being a millionaire before age forty. Then there are the constant studies that put a dollar figure on the value of different university degrees in terms of income and net worth levels. Yes the goal to be rich is very much alive in our society. However, a follow up on MBA graduates would show some disappointments. They quickly discover that choosing a course is no guarantee of success. It might be argued that the greater desire for riches, the greater risk of failure. When we feel pressured to accumulate a large retirement fund we are more likely to take risk, rationalizing that the greater the risk —— the greater the reward. As has been recently demonstrated in the equity market, there is the other side of the coin: the greater opportunity to lose all or much of your savings and arrive next door to me. Of course you won't be comfortable being my neighbour; you had your sights on the fast lane.

But occasionally, someone will pursue wealth and actually catch it. Then he could be living in the fast lane, complete with fast cars and big houses, paying security firms to guard all his toys, paying insurance companies to replace the toys when they are stolen, paying gardeners, maintenance workers, mechanics and carpenters to maintain the toys so they would look good enough to steal, paying big taxes, hiring lawyers and accountants for big money, so that they too can have all the toys and pay big taxes and....

If that sounds like more fun than lying in a hammock under an apple tree watching the grandkids chasing butterflies, you probably don't own a hammock.

About the Author

Alan Dickson has been a bank employee, janitor, restaurant owner, sign maker, window tinter, and insurance and investment salesman.

He is often asked why he likes to be called a "recovering financial planner"?

"It's not a good idea to take yourself too seriously, nobody else does. I thought it would be fun to look at this scheming to acquire huge retirement funds as more of an addiction than a profession. We all know people who are addicted to money — they can never get enough."

With the success of his first book *Free Parking*, Alan has added 'author' to his resume`.

He prefers to be known as a husband and father. He lives with his wife, Debra and their youngest daughter Emily in Duncan, British Columbia.

You can reach Alan at:

www.freemoneypress.com
870 Government Street
Duncan, B.C. V9L 1B6
(250) 748-7032

BOOK ORDERS

Please send me _____ copies of *Free Parking*

_____ copies of *Advance To Go*

@ $19.95 ($14.95 U.S.) plus $3.00 s/h. Orders of two or more copies are shipped free of charge. Canadian residents please add 7% GST

Name _____

Address _____

_____

_____

Phone # _____

E-mail _____

Please send cheque or money order to:

Preferred Marketing Inc.
870 Government St.
Duncan, B.C. V9L 1B6
www.freemoneypress.com